Stormy Weather

Rev. Darryl Mark Matthews

FREE STORMY WEATHER DEVOTIONAL

Thanks for purchasing this book. I know that it will be a blessing in your life. To further enhance your walk with Christ, I want to bless you with a 30-Day Stormy Weather Devotional Journal.

Just visit

www.stormyweatherbook.com/devotions or bit.ly/2pARnO4

Stormy Weather

Darryl M Matthews

www.stormyweatherbook.com

Published by Vital Living Media LLC
1st Edition
First published in 2017

ISBN-13: 978-0-9989-7430-9

ISBN-10: 0998974307

Vital Living Media LLC
Riverview FL
United States of America

Website: www.stormyweatherbook.com
Email: revmatthews@stormyweatherbook.com
Office: 813-413-1680

DEDICATION

This book is dedicated to my beloved father, Dr. Verner R. Matthews (1923-2001). Thanks Dad for making such a significant investment in my life and modeling the servant-like character of Jesus Christ before me throughout your life.

TABLE OF CONTENTS

ACKNOWLEDGMENTS i

INTRODUCTION iii

1 WITHOUT WARNING...1

    Storms Can Arise Without Warning 4

    Make Sure You're Following Jesus 8

    Make Sure Jesus Is Still On Board 10

        Prayer..14

        Journal Reflections..15

2 WHEN GOD IS SILENT..16

    Silence Tests Us..20

    Silence Challenges Our Memory 22

    Silence Challenges Our Status...................................29

        Prayer..33

        Reflection Questions...34

3 DEALING WITH FEAR...35

    Fear Loves Ignorance 39

    Fear Loves Isolation 43

    Fear Has To Submit To Prayer....................................47

        Reflection Questions...54

4 JESUS SAVES...56

    Our Faith Is Supposed To Grow 58

    Why Be Afraid? 61

Jesus Can Handle The Storm 63

    Reflection Questions..66

5 LESSONS LEARNED 68

We Need To Appreciate What God Has Done 71

We Have To Ask The Right Questions 74

Experience Leads To Worship 76

    Reflection Questions..80

ABOUT THE AUTHOR..82

REVIEW REQUEST 83

ACKNOWLEDGMENTS

No book is written in isolation but is a collaboration with a number of people and such is the case with this my first book. Thanks must first be given to my Lord and Savior Jesus Christ who took me through a storm I didn't want to go through and brought me through.

I am forever grateful for my dedicated and supportive wife Jowancia who gave me the time and the space to craft this text as well as much prayer and encouragement along the way.

I've wanted to produce a book for a number of years. In fact, this should not have been my first book. But the person who lite a fire under me to create this first full manuscript was Dr Leslie Devereaux through her Book In Your Belly webinar. I am grateful to Dr Leslie for walking me through the concept and writing phases of this book in 2016. Her encouragement and experience was invaluable.

The writing process is not complete without someone reviewing and editing the manuscript and that task fell upon my Malawi missionary friend Leslie Christian of Oklahoma. She took the time to read through my rough draft and not only corrected my grammar and phrasing but gave me some helpful feedback on the effectiveness of the text itself and I am so thankful for her hard work and her friendship.

Pastor Brett Snowden of the Greater Bethel Baptist Church of Tampa also reviewed some of the manuscript as well and offered some excellent insight.

Finally, I am thankful for the St Mark Missionary Baptist Church which gave me the opportunity to first craft and preach the messages which would become the basis for this book.

.

INTRODUCTION

Every book comes out of some kind of context and such is the case with this volume. This book is the outgrowth of a sermon series that I had the privilege of preaching at a time in my life when I was going through some stormy weather. It wasn't a storm of my choosing and I didn't welcome it and didn't want to go through it but it was a storm that I had go through anyway.

I was pastoring a Baptist church in South Florida and had been giving leadership in that fellowship for over five years. In the month prior to commencing this sermon series I thought that ministry at this fellowship was going pretty good as pastoring goes. As has been my custom for a number of years I made a pilgrimage to the country of Malawi--warm heart of Africa—for an annual mission trip. This trip was very rewarding and a blessing to me as it had been for the last couple of years.

I returned from the African continent and ran smack into a storm. All of a sudden the Deacon board that I thought I was on good relations with were asking for my resignation not because of any misconduct on my part or some heinous act that I had done. Discussions about my continued pastorate at this church went on for the next two months before the church meeting that was convened to vote me up or down. Ultimately the deacons convinced a majority of the congregation that my ministry to that body of Christ was no longer welcomed and I was dismissed immediately.

The sermon series "Handling The Storms of Life" was preached during period when I was going through the deliberations with the deacons and the church body. The experience of the disciples and Jesus on the Sea of Galilee was something similar to what I was experiencing at this time in my life. I was going along doing ministry and enjoying pastoring when out of the blue a storm rose up (Chapter 1 – Without Warning).

It was a storm that I did not see coming and it jumped up so suddenly that it blindsided me. I am not one of those pastor/teachers who arrogantly holds authority and power over the people I have been entrusted to serve so I didn't understand why I was going through this season. I prayed at times talking with the Lord attempting to find some answers to why I was going down this path without getting too many satisfying answers (Chapter 2 – When God Is Silent).

I didn't know how this storm was going to turn out but I did know that I was going to stand my ground and ask the deacons to make their case to the congregation and then vote me up or down. I didn't know what the outcome of that church meeting was going to be (Chapter 3 – Dealing With Fear) but I went in with the calm assurance that Jesus was still the captain of my ship.

The fact that Jesus Saved (Chapter 4) the disciples in the

midst of the storm might lead you to think that Jesus saved me in the pastorate. That didn't happen but it was not the end of the story in my life. It just meant that my service at that Baptist church had come to an end. As the Lord would have it, another door was opened after that release. A door where my gifts and talents were welcomed. Like the disciples I had to review and unpack the entire experience and see what Lessons I Could Learn (Chapter 5) from the storm through which I had come.

I am grateful to God for what I went through. I have forgiven the deacons and members in that church that dismissed me. God called home one of the deacons that called for my resignation. I've had to work through some of the emotions and heat of the situation but the Holy Spirit has ministered to me.

I hope that my experience will give you some encouragement to go through the storms that come your way in life and learn some important lessons that will power you forward and upward. There is nothing to be gained from complaining about the storm or trying to avoid the storms that come our way. We all are going to have to through them. As you read the following pages, learn to go through them knowing that Jesus hasn't left us and that there are some things we can learn in Stormy Weather

1 WITHOUT WARNING

We begin our journey in 8th chapter of the book of Matthew, the first book of the NT. Our focus throughout the book will center on Matthew 8:23-27 (NIV).

> Matthew 8:23–27, 23Then he got into the boat and his disciples followed him. 24Without warning, a furious storm came up on the lake, so that the waves swept over the boat. But Jesus was sleeping. 25The disciples went and woke him, saying, "Lord, save us! We're going to drown!" 26He replied, "You of little faith, why are you so afraid?" Then he got up and rebuked the winds and the waves, and it was completely calm. 27The men were amazed and asked, "What kind of man is this? Even the winds and the waves obey him!"

Our focus in this chapter is on vs 23-24, "Then he got into the boat and his disciples followed him. 24Without warning, a furious storm came up on the lake, so that the waves swept over the boat."

As we'll do with each chapter, let's begin with a word of prayer,

> "Thank you dear Lord for your Word. Where would we be without your Word? The psalmist says that it is a lamp unto our feed and light unto our footsteps. Gracious Lord, we pray that you would hide your word in our hearts that we might not sin against you. Gracious Lord we thank You for the effect that this chapter will have in the life of this dear reader. Bless us in the most powerful way we pray in the name of Him that is King of Kings and Lord of Lords, Jesus Christ, Amen."

Storms by their very nature are disruptive. You go to the beach ready to take on the day and have fun in the sun. You have your sun block on along with your bikini or swimming suit and you're ready to go. You have your little cabana set up and maybe you even took your hibachi grill with you and you are ready to have a good time on the beach, but just as soon as you get settled, you notice some storm clouds start to float into your line of sight and you get the feeling that your lovely plans for the beach are about to be disrupted.

Or maybe you've experience the situation where you go in the mall to do some shopping and it's a bright sunshiny day when you pulled into the parking lot. There is not even a hint that anything was going to happen as you walk into the mall. But when you come out you recognize that not only is the rain falling, but you left your umbrella in the car. Now you are faced with the prospect of either doing more shopping (and spending money you didn't intend on spending) or walking in the rain without an umbrella and getting soaked. You went in dry but now you are riding home soaking wet and the first signs of a cold are showing up.

Or maybe you've been down this road before: You are going on a trip and you make your way to the airport so that you will be on hand way in advance of the scheduled departure time. My wife, Jowancia, experienced this one summer when she was traveling to Washington DC for a brief vacation with her mom.

She was ready to departure from Tampa International but she couldn't leave when she was supposed to because the plane that was scheduled to take her to the nation's capital hadn't arrived in Tampa yet. What was the cause of the delay? A storm had arisen in North Carolina and delayed the plane from taking off there and making its way to Tampa. Until the plane arrived in Tampa there was no way my wife was going to begin her vacation. The storm in North Carolina disrupted her best laid plans in Florida.

Regular storms are bothersome enough yet there are the storms that are downright destructive. Living in south Florida, I have come to understand that between June and October, we can have hurricane-type winds come that can level whole communities. On March 11, 2013, an earthquake shook the ocean floor off of Japan and caused a tsunami that struck the coastal cities of Japan. That wall of destructive water picked up cars and tractor trailers and threw them around like they were toy vehicles. Some storms are just destructive.

And if the actual storms were not bad enough, sometimes in our personal lives we have storms that arise that are just as disruptive, destructive, and memorable. As we begin our journey through this passage in Matthew, it all begins with Jesus and the disciples encountering a storm as they cross the sea of Galilee.

Try as we might to avoid storms in our lives, you and I are going to have some bad weather. A wise clergyman has said that either you are in a storm; you are coming out of a storm; or you're headed into a storm. John said in the gospel of John, "In this world you will have trouble . . ." so our time spent throughout the course of this book is on a topic that all of us will have to face problems in our lives at some point.

Storms Can Arise Without Warning

Jesus and the disciples have just completed a massive healing campaign earlier in the chapter in verses 5-17. Jesus has been healing folks who had infirmities in their bodies and He was touching them and bringing healing in the lives of individuals who were sick. Following the healing sessions, Jesus has some conversations with some would be followers who display varying degrees of commitment to following Jesus. After He gets done with those conversations, he directs the disciples to get into a boat and cross the lake. This journey should have been a routine trip like so many others the disciples had taken in their lives. But then v. 24 comes onto the scene, ". . . without warning . . ."

Storms have a way of crashing into our lives without any advance notice. One moment you are having the time of your live with your loved one and suddenly a heart attack or a stroke pop up and "BAM" they are gone without notice. You're riding along one day and things are going well, the next thing you know the car is flipping without notice because a drunk driver has struck you. That child of yours that seemed to be walking in the light of all those years of Sunday School, Worship and AWANA, all of a sudden lands in jail without any kind of warning or advance notice.

These storms pop up without any advance notice of their coming. Like when you park your car in one spot at the mall or supermarket, you go into the mall or grocery store to do your shopping only to come back out and discover that the vehicle is missing. It's been stolen. Talk about a feeling. Without notice! The burglar didn't say, "Can I have your permission to take your vehicle?"

Have you ever had the experience where you just got paid and you go to the grocery store and you take out your debit card to swipe it and you hear that short staccato buzz from the machine? "Try again" the cashier says. "Try it by credit". Still no success. You know you just got paid. That's a storm that has popped up out of nowhere and caused you to feel like crawling up under a rock.

Storms have a way of coming up in our lives without any kind of advance warning. They are just rude like that. What makes them so devastating is the fact that we don't know even know that they are on the way. As much as we like to think we know what's going to happen tomorrow, we really don't know. If we are honest with ourselves, we really don't know what is going to happen in the next few moments. Do you think that anyone going to work in either of the twin towers on the morning of September 11, 2001 thought that that morning would be the last sunrise they would see? Storms can rise up quickly, disrupt our routine and cause a lot of devastation all without announcement.

As believers, a positive disruption would be if Jesus Christ were to break through the clouds and take us back to glory with Him.   Even His return is not known by anyone except our Heavenly Father. We can plan for tomorrow but Jesus could come before you even finish reading this sentence (still here? Ok, let's press on then).

We really don't know what's going to happen from one moment to the next. Consider the biblical testimony of a man called Job. Tell us Job what happened in your life. "One afternoon I was sitting in my home enjoying the day when all of a sudden I got a report that my oxen in the field and the donkey's that were grazing nearby were taken by some thieves who not only stole my livestock but also killed my faithful employees. As if that wasn't bad enough another messenger comes in right behind the first one and tells me that fire fell from the sky and burned up my sheep and the shepherds that were taking care of them. Wiped them out completely. And if those two things weren't bad enough, the Chaldeans came and formed a raiding party and stole all my camels.

"To compound the situation further, my family was then touched. My children were gathered at my eldest son's house for a get together and I received a report from a servant at the house that the winds came, blew in the house and now all my offspring are dead. Just like that my legacy was gone. All this happened in one afternoon and I didn't know any of it was coming."

What we need to understand is that storms not only come without invitation but they also are unavoidable. When the storm shows up on your doorstep, you need to be prepared already. The storm might be passing over but it is still coming. When they strike, they tend to hit you are right then and there's no getting around the storm.

Have you ever watched the storm chasers on television? You and I try to stay away from tornados but they relish the thought of tracking one down. Sometimes, they think they know what they are doing. They are running around all over OK and the Midwest. At times it looks like the storm is headed on a certain track, but a storm can turn on a dime and if they are too close, they may not get a chance to get out of its way.

We need to understand that storms are going to come in our lives without invitation for as long as we have breath in our body. There is not going to be a time when we will be storm free. There may be those moments coming out of bad weather that things can be calm and even in the midst of a hurricane at sea, you can get some calmness when you reach the eye of the storm, but for the most part there is no way to avoid the tempests that ultimately will arise.

Jesus said, "In this world you will have trouble." When the prosperity gospel preacher comes to you and says that everything should be sunshine and roses, you just need ask them, "What did Jesus mean when he said we'd have trouble?" My bible tells me IN THIS WORLD, not the world to come; not some other dimension but IN THIS WORLD you and I would have trouble. Job in his testimony says, "Man that is born of a woman is but of a few days and FULL of trouble."

So the fact that we have storms and that they come without warning might prompt you ask, "Preacher what am I supposed to do? You're telling me the strong gales are coming my way but what am I supposed to do when a they pop up in my life?" No matter when they come or how large or small the storm may be, do these two things and you can make to through the squall: (1) Make sure you're following Jesus and (2) Make sure that Jesus is still on board.

Make Sure You're Following Jesus

Sometimes when we read the scriptures we run right past some verses kind of lightly but don't miss v. 23, "Then He [talking about Jesus] got into the boat AND His disciples followed him." See before there was a v. 24 ("without warning") there was a v. 23 ("his disciples followed him"). The disciples were in the place where Jesus had led them. We have to give the disciples some credit as they sometimes get a bad rap for their lack of faith and sometimes they question what Jesus is doing, but here they did follow Jesus. Not everyone is willing to follow Jesus.

When you dial back a couple of verses in this chapter and look at v 18-22, Jesus has a couple of conversations with people about the costs of following Jesus. Some people are just vocal believers. They talk a good game, but when it really comes to actually following Jesus, their talk and their walk don't match up. You see there in v. 18 one said, "Lord wherever you are going I'm going to be with you." Jesus said, "You said that you were going to follow me but foxes have holes and birds have nests but I don't have any of that to offer you right now."

Jesus lets this would be follower know that if he intends on following Jesus just for the benefits, he should reconsider his reasons for signing up. If we are going to follow Jesus, it should be because of our love for Him and for where it is that Jesus wants to take us and not for material gain. Matthew 6:33 tells us to focus on God's kingdom agenda first and all the things we need for this life will be given to us on the journey.

There are some believers who will say like the second man Jesus encountered in Matt 8:xx, "Lord I'll be with you BUT let me check my schedule and see if I can walk with

8

you; let me make sure that I can walk with you this week" (Matthews paraphrase). But Jesus said, "I don't know what's on your agenda but let the dead go bury the dead." Some say I'm on the Lord's side on Sunday or when the preacher is around but when its not Sunday and the preacher is not around they say, "I'm on my own time." But true discipleship isn't dependent upon other believers being around or it being convenient but true discipleship is when one is faithful to their profession regardless of the circumstances. It's not just saying "Jesus I'll follow you" and then wave "Bon voyage" as they pull off from the shore.

If you are follower of Christ then you're going to get in the boat. Why? Because wherever Jesus is going is the place where you should want to be. You might be, "That's all well and good but did Jesus want the disciples to be in the storm?" It's not a matter of avoiding the uproar but to understand that this gale arose in the context of the disciples following Jesus. That's the point to take away from this passage.

The storm came as they were following Jesus. Some religious leaders of the day would tell you that if you are following Jesus that everything should just be tip toe through the tulips and that life should be without pain. You should have a house in Beverly Hills and that servants should be at your beck and call all over the residence. But if you follow Jesus, He's going to will take you some places that are not sunshine and roses.

Just because you're a child of God doesn't mean that monsoons will not arise up in your life. When they do arise, you need to check and make sure that they came up while you were following Jesus. Because if you're following Jesus and you come up against a storm, then Jesus can sustain you IN the storm. More in future chapters, but if you're following Jesus then Romans 8:28 becomes activated, "All things work together for good to those who love Him and have been called according to his purpose."

Now, if you're in a storm and it happened when you decided to go your own way instead of following Jesus, you are in a perilous situation. If you end up in a storm and you are doing it on your own, then you're out there by yourself. That is not a good place to be. So, when the storms come up in your life, check to see if you've been walking the path that Jesus has laid out for you. Make sure that you've been following Jesus.

Make Sure Jesus Is Still On Board

We are prone, when the storms of life pop up, to focus on the storm. When your doctor tells you that you have cancer, all of your attention gets focused on the sickness and the different treatments that are available. When the boss calls you in and says that they have to reduce the workforce and that includes you, all of your attention, if you're not careful, gets focused on how you're going to make ends meet. When that spouse that you have been with for 20-30 years says that "its over," all of your attention can become focused on how you're going to life live without them.

The disciples were focused on the size of the waves. V. 24 says that these were not just small waves. My wife and I love to go on cruises. We've been blessed to travel to a number places throughout the Caribbean and when we are on the boat, there are many a wave that bounce up against the ship and there is never a problems so long as the waves are just bouncing up against the ship. There is no problem with waves hitting the hull of the ship because when you're out in the water on a boat, that is what waves are supposed to do.

But a problem arises when the water starts coming into the ship! These weren't just some small waves the disciples were encountering but the text says that the water was sweeping over the sides of the boat meaning the disciples were probably taking on some water. I don't know about you but when I'm out on the water in a boat, I expect the water to stay where the water is and not to be in the boat. When the water decides that it wants to get in the boat, then we have a crisis on our hands.

When the storms do pop up in your life don't focus on the storm but just check to make sure that Jesus is still on board in your life. If you have been following Jesus and you are where He is, then Jesus is on board. The text says, ". . . but Jesus was sleeping." Don't fret that Jesus is sleeping. It is alright that he was sleeping. The key factor is that He is still on board. He might not be awake but that's alright, he's still on board.

Are you trying to fix the situation yourself? Don't yield to that temptation. Check and see if Jesus is on board. Are you calling everyone on the phone talking about the storm and describing the storm and saying, "I'm not ready for the storm"? You should be checking to see if Jesus is still on board. Instead of trying to figure who can bail you out and calling your other stormy friends and saying, "sista gurl can you hand me a pail and come on over and help me bail some water?" No, check and see if Jesus is still on board.

As believers what we need to do is look for Jesus in every situation. Proverbs 3:6 says, "In all your ways acknowledge Him . . ." That is your queue to include Jesus in every aspect of your life. If Jesus is on board your ship, everything is going to be alright. The boat might fill up with water but it is not going to sink. Why? Because Jesus is on board. The storm may even intensify but that's alright, Jesus is on board. The sun might refuse to shine but that's alright because Jesus is on board. Might have to cry sometimes but that's alright because Jesus is on board. You might have to go through the storm by yourself when others have jumped ship but that's alright because Jesus is still on board. Might have to endure some embarrassment sometime but that is not a problem because Jesus is on board.

As a child of God, when Jesus is on the ship only so much can happen. Why? Because He is King of kings and Lord of Lords. When Jesus is on board, the storm can only do much. I like what the hymn writer said, "Like a ship that's tossed and driven. Battered by an angry sea. When the storms of life are raging, and their fury falls on me. I wonder what I have done, that makes this race so hard to run. Then I say to my soul, "Take courage," I don't know how the Lord is going to do it. I don't know how he's gong to work it out. He looks like he's sleeping right now so I don't know how he's going to work it out but I know, "the Lord will make a way somehow."

"Try to do my best in service, try to do the best I can. When I choose to do the right thing evil's present on every hand." Seems like my neighbor that's not serving God is driving a Mercedes and eating filet mignon and living in a big house while I'm just making it on franks and beans and driving a hoopty. "I look up and wonder why that good fortune passed me by. Then I say to my soul, "Be patient, the Lord will make a way somehow."

"The Lord will make a way somehow when beneath the cross I bow. He will take away each sorrow; let Him. . ." That's the problem we don't let him. But you have to "let him have your burdens now. When the load . . ." I don't know about you but storms have a way of putting a load on you. ". . . bears down so heavy the weight is shown upon my brow. There's a sweet relief in knowing the Lord will make a way somehow."

You might be reading this today and you know what its like to go through storms. Maybe you haven't just sung, The Lord Will Make A Way Somehow but you have lived that song. If so, then you know that storms are real and that the Lord will make a way out of no way.

Storms are going to come. There's no avoiding them. You're going to have to go through a storm sometime in your life. It's not a matter of "if" but "when." Jesus came into this world so that you and I don't have to go through these storms by ourselves. He paid the price for our sins at calvary. Why? So we wouldn't have to try to figure out this getting to God on our own. If you've never accepted Christ in the pardon of your sins, then you are trying to make it through life's storms with your own resources and that's a perilous situation to be in. You need to know that Jesus is on board and that he's the captain of your ship.

God has thrown out a lifeline to anyone who will believe. The Bible says that ". . . God so loved the world that he gave is only begotten son. That whosoever believeth in Him should not perish but have everlasting life." As you are reading this book now, you may not be in the storm. Maybe you're headed towards one. Recognize that storms can come without warning. You're not going to know when they are coming. You have to adopt the Boy Scout motto, "Be prepared."

You know that they are coming. They can pop up when you least expect them. Isn't that the very nature of a storm? Crises are the same way in our lives? If it were up to you and I, we would never have a crisis? If it were up to us we'd say, "Lord don't ever touch my <you fill in the blank>. I believe in you, I'm trusting you for eternity. Take me home but please don't put me through any tests." But that's not how life is. God says its testing time and sometimes He allows the storms of life to come and they hit us.

Until you receive Jesus on the inside, those storms will just toss you to and fro. But if you've got Jesus on the inside; if you've got his word on the inside, then you can sing that old song, "My anchor holds and grips the solid rock." Let us recognize that storms will pop up without warning. Read on to the next chapter to see how Jesus deals with these storms.

Prayer

Thank you Lord for the storms that have come up in our lives. Oh dear Lord if it were up to us we wouldn't ask for the storms. We don't like storms. We like sunshine Lord. We like it when it is easy but gracious Lord storms challenge us. Dear Lord, storms are going to come because of this sin filled world in which we live. But gracious Lord we thank you that you haven't left us by ourselves. You haven't left it up to us to figure out how to get through the storms but you came down and made a way. You showed us how to walk, to talk and then went to the cross so that we might know how to live day by day. That when the storms of life come our way, we can hold on to your word and hold on to you. Hold on to the Holy Spirit who is on the inside of each and every one of us. There may be some reading or listening right now who has never accepted Jesus Christ. They talk about how they are following him but they are still on the shore after the boat has set sail. Gracious Father, I pray even right now that your Holy Spirit would do a work in the life of that man or woman that doesn't know Jesus in the pardon of their sins.

That they might come crying even right now, "I'm not going to try to make it through this life by myself. I need Jesus on the inside." May the Holy Spirit draw them even right now. Thank you for the tempests you have brought us through because they built our faith. Thank you for the gales we went through because we have a better testimony as to what you can do in our lives. Oh gracious Lord, we just thank you right now, I pray that you would keep us in the days and weeks ahead. For we pray these things in Jesus name. Amen.

Journal Reflections

1. Jot down three or four incidents in your life where a storm arose in your life quickly and without   warning.

2. What were your initial reactions to the storm? Were they positive or negative? Did you receive the storm as a potential learning experience?

3. Did you pray in the midst of the storm? What were the nature/contents of those prayers?

4. What life lessons did you learn coming out of the storm? What did you learn about God after coming through the storm? Have you been able to bless others who have gone through a similar storm?

2 WHEN GOD IS SILENT

The gospel according to St Matthew 8:23-27

> Matthew 8:23–27,23 Then he got into the boat
> and his disciples followed him. 24 Suddenly a
> furious storm came up on the lake, so that the
> waves swept over the boat. But Jesus was sleeping.
> 25 The disciples went and woke him, saying,
> "Lord, save us! We're going to drown!" 26 He
> replied, "You of little faith, why are you so
> afraid?" Then he got up and rebuked the winds
> and the waves, and it was completely calm. 27 The
> men were amazed and asked, "What kind of man
> is this? Even the winds and the waves obey him!"

Our focus for this chapter is the later part of v. 24, ". . .
But Jesus was sleeping." Jesus was sleeping. Let us pray,

> Gracious Lord we thank you for your word. Your
> word is truth. Your word is a lamp unto our feet

and a light unto our footsteps. Gracious Lord, I pray even now that you open the eyes of my brother or sister reading and that your Holy Spirit would use this text for your glory and your honor. May this chapter give clarity where there is a lack of focus. Speak to our hearts right now, dear Jesus, for your servants are listening. This is your servant's prayer in Jesus name, Amen.

Have you ever experienced the silent treatment from someone? If you have been married or in a relationship with a significant other, then there have probably been sometimes when you have experienced the silent treatment. Maybe as a husband you did something that you should not have done. Maybe one day you said something that you should not have said and all of a sudden that lovely bride that is normally talkative and is interacting with you gets quiet. Right then and there you know something is wrong. You ask a question and all you get back is crickets. The silent treatment can be hard to endure and overcome.

Sometimes, it's difficult when someone gives you the silent treatment. It can be unnerving because most people have to have some kind of noise around them 24 hours a day, 7 days a week. Some people cannot even sleep at night unless a radio is on or a television is on because they have become so used to having some kind of audible stimuli in their lives. Silence bothers us because silence sometimes reminds us that we are alone and we do not like being alone.

 It is one thing to get the silent treatment from a human being but what happens when it appears that God is being silent with us? What happens when you are going through a stormy period in your life and it would appear that God is not even responding to you? You fast and you pray and the answer appears to be slow in coming or not at all. You have prayers going up and down the prayer chain. You have prayer circles all over the place praying for you and yet, still no solution appears to be on the horizon.

You may have gotten so desperate that you sent in your $25 donation to the prayer club or sent for some kind of prayer cloth from a television evangelist that is supposed to have blessings coming your way and even though you've done that, your blessing still hasn't shown up. You are still in the storm.

In the passage before us in this chapter, we return to the scene of the Sea of Galilee with Jesus and the disciples already in the midst of the storm. Storm clouds have transformed what should have been a routine crossing into a very harrowing experience. The water is sweeping into the boat faster than it can be emptied out. And yet, look at what Jesus is doing in the midst of all this commotion: He is sleeping!

How is it that the King of kings and Lord of Lords is fast asleep? Jesus is sleeping because while He was on this Earth, not only was He all God, but He was all human as well. Jesus was the God-Man and as a human being, this body gets tired. You can only go so long in this flesh without getting some rest.

In the 1950s, there was a movie with Kevin McCarthy called Invasion of the Body Snatchers. Aliens came to earth but could only take over your body when you went to sleep. The problem for our heroes in the movie was that one could only stay awake so long before you succumbed to the overwhelming urge to fall asleep and then you were doomed. As human beings we can only go so long before this body gets tired.

So, Jesus was sleeping because he was tired. Jesus was tired because He had just come off of a major Kingdom Agenda conference. Matthew 5-7 captures Jesus seminar on the Christian Life that we call The Sermon On The Mount. Matthew 5:1 says, "Now when Jesus saw the crowds, he went up on a mountainside and sat down . . ." Jesus had to hike "up on a mountainside" and even if it wasn't a large mountain, there was some climbing involved a certain amount of physical energy.

Once Jesus found the right place to begin his teaching, He proceeded to teach the people for a long period of time. Jesus covered all the material between Matthew 5 and 7 (remember that chapters were added to the scriptures by scholars many years later). Preaching and teaching can be hard work and Jesus' teaching was so well received that large crowds started following Him everywhere.

Jesus comes out of the Christian Life Conference in Matthew 7 right into a healing campaign in the early part of Matthew 8 that included lepers (8:1-4), a Roman centurion's servant (8:5-13), Peter's mother-in-law (8:14-15) and a demon possessed man (8:16-17). He then challenges some would be followers before making the choice to cross the Sea of Galilee. The boat probably represented a chance for Jesus to rest. An opportunity to rest for a good while and totally uninterrupted by the crowds and the demands of His flourishing ministry.

So, Jesus is asleep on board the boat and unaware that a storm has risen or that the boat is taking on water. Water is coming over the edge and Jesus is sleeping. Waves are rocking the boat violently back and forth to the point where the disciples are yelling out in desperation but Jesus is sleeping. Jesus sleeping was Him being silent in the midst of a harrowing situation. Maybe you are reading this today and a storm is swirling in your life. It may appear that all the resources of Heaven have all of a sudden gone dark. All the resources of glory have dropped off the radar and somehow it seems like your calls aren't being taken.

Even though you are going through the storm and you feel like you're all alone, there is a word of encouragement that we can glean from this passage. There are some lessons that we can learn for our Christian life when God appears to be silent.

Silence Tests Us

Silence has a way of testing us. A faith that is not tested becomes weak and ineffective. Just like the muscles in our body, if you don't use them on a regular basis, they become weak and flimsy. We have been led to believe sometimes in the Christian faith that God is at OUR beck and call. Sometimes, we think that God exists to meet our needs.

Look at how often we sing, "I'm looking for a miracle." If we are not careful, one could come to the conclusion that miracles are poured out as an everyday occurrence. Even in the Word of God, miracles came every now and then. It would appear they came more frequently but a careful reading of the people of God in the Bible yields miracles being every now and then. But, in this day and age some believers are being misled to think that God's purpose is to do something solely for me, myself and I.

Look at what else we sing, "Jesus is on the mainline. Tell him what you want.". The last time I checked, when you are on a phone it is a two way communication avenue; not only do you speak but you also hear—so if Jesus is on the mainline, then not only am I talking to Him and sharing what is on my mind but Jesus might have something that He wants to say to me as well while He's got me on the line.

Have you ever run into some who, when you start talking to them, you can't get a word into the conversation? You call them up and say "hi' and you can't get a word into the conversation for twenty minutes because they keep going on and on and on and on. It is almost as if they don't even stop to take a breath! That's how it is with us and our conversation with God at times. "Go here" and "go there" and "Lord bless me with . . ." and "Lord see about . . ."

We have been led as believers (at least in our singing) to believe that God exists to respond to us. Now understand, God is able to do all things. The emphasis on some of the songs we sing is more about US than about God. Too many times our devotion to God is based on what God is doing for us rather than what we are doing for God. It is almost like we've taken up the popular song that Janet Jackson sang years ago, "What Have You Done For Me Lately?"

It's a very arrogant spirit that says if God hasn't done anything for me lately, then I don't have to do anything for God. The emphasis in our lives should be about what we are doing for God. Jesus sacrificed his life on the cross at Calvary giving each and every one of us who believed eternal life. If God doesn't do another thing for us in this life, God's done enough right there! The fact that he died on the cross for your sins and my sins ought to be enough by itself. God has blessed us and already done more than enough.

But storms have a way of bringing some clarity back into the picture. Silences definitely has a way of testing our faith. What was Job's biggest dilemma? It wasn't the fact that he lost all of his earthly possessions. It wasn't the fact that his children died. The thing that bothered Job the most was that he was in the midst of a storm and he was looking for heaven; looking above for God and was not hearing anything. He says, "Lord why do you hide your face and consider me your enemy?" That's what Job was going through in the midst of his storm. He was saying, "Why Lord? I need you and you've hidden your face from me." Even David records in Psalms 22 his desire to hear from God in the midst of trouble yet he was hearing nothing but silence, "My God, I cry out by day, but you do not answer, by night, but I find no rest" (v. 2).

Storms have a way of testing our faith. Will we be faithful to God even when we don't hear from God? Will we continue to walk the narrow path even when God is not showering us with blessings? Or are you the kind of believer that God's got to be at your beck and call all the time for you to be faithful? Are you a battle tested believer or a fair weather friend? Silence tests our faith and trust in the Lord.

Silence Challenges Our Memory

Silence not only tests our faith but it challenges our memory as well. Many times in the storm we are looking for a revelation from God to guide and direct us. Even if God never speaks during the storm, God has already spoken volumes to us. The question is, "Have we listened?" As parents, we know what it's like to speak and not be heard. We speak a lot of things to our children. We say things over and over and over again and yet sometimes they go off somewhere, hear another voice from someone else who repeats the same things we've been telling them and those jokers come back with this great revelation as if they have just gotten some NEW information. "Mom,

Dad, listen to what I just learned from so and so . . ." All you can do is shake your head and say, "I've been telling you that all along and the questions is, 'Have you been listening?'"

When we don't hear from God or it appears that God is silent, you need to have a reservoir from which you can draw. Do you have a deep reservoir of God's Word that's stored up in your spirit?

I live in the hurricane prone area of south Florida. When storms are forecasted here, people start scrambling to go to Home Depot and get the shutters and plywood needed to put on your window. The problem is that when the storm is announced, everyone and their brother will be making runs to Home Depots and Lowe's all over the place and you might not get what you really need when the storm is coming. You can wait until the storm is announced but you may not get what you need in time for the drops of water.

It is far better to have what you need on hand when the forecast is given than to try to pull thing together at the last minute. When I moved into my new home in 2013, there were these long aluminum strut looking things propped up against the wall in my garage. At first, I thought the builders had left some scaffolding behind and just forgot to collect it. When we got to the closing on the house, I found out that the "scaffolding" were not forgotten building materials, but were shutters that are supposed to cover my windows in case a hurricane. What I needed for the storm was already in place and ready ahead of the stormy event!

When you are in the midst of the storm, you can try to get ready for the storm when it hits, but it is much better if you are already prepared for the storm before the storm strikes. How many times in our churches do pastors and superintendents implore people to come to Sunday School, come to Bible Study, be a part of the local Association's seminars and classes? Why the constant invitations? So that you can get the Word of God down into your spirit ahead of time.

You need to get the Word of God into your spirit on a regular basis because, as I tried to impress upon you in Chapter 1, the storms are going to come. Maybe you are not in a storm right now but you just keep on living. Remember that storms do not send you a "save the date".

Storms are going to come. And when they do show up, you need to be READY before they even hits. You need to get into the habit now of putting yourself in a position where you can get the Word down into your soul ahead of the storm. When you expose yourself to good Bible teaching on a regular basis, you are allowing the word to marinate over your spirit and soak down into your spirit to the point that it becomes a part of you.

When I was attending seminary in Washington, D.C., I purchased a used Saturn sedan that had a manual stick shift transmission. For over twenty years I had been driving an automatic car so when I obtained this car with a manual stick transmission, every driving experience was a deliberate exercise in "clutch, shift, clutch, shift, clutch, shift." Traffic was never a problem with the automatic transmission but now it was laborious with the stick. Eating and driving had never been a challenge before with the automatic but it is hard to "clutch, shift" with a burger in your hand.

I continued to make the trip from York, PA to Washington, DC over the three years of seminary sometimes three or four times a week passing through

Baltimore's inner harbor on my way to the nation's capital and as I went through the traffic and the by ways down to DC, I learned how to "clutch, shift" to the point that I no longer had to think about the driving experience. I just got in the car and took off. The process of driving was soaked into my being, so that I didn't have to think about it any more.

When we absorb the power of God's word in our lives regularly, it becomes second nature for us to lean and depend on God even when heaven appears to be silent. Job declared, "All the days of my hired service, I'm going to wait until my change comes." (Job 14:14) The pslamist says, "Some trust in chariots and some trust in horses but I will trust in the name of the Lord our God" (Psalms 20:7). "When I am afraid, I will trust in you" (Psalms 56:3). What can mortal man do to God's child? You need to store up strength for the journey on the inside. "The Lord is my rock and my fortress, my deliver. My God is my rock in whom I take refuge. He is my shield and my horn. My stronghold" (Psalms 18:2). You have to get God's word down into your soul. That's what Jesus was talking about in his sermon on the mount when he said that if you have God's word, you are like a man who build his house on the solid rock. Winds can blow and the rains can come but you will be able to stand strong because your life is built upon the solid foundation of God's Word.

Do you have a rich storehouse? Do you have anything residing within the grey matter between your ears? We carry so much information in our heads don't we? In fact, some have information that they really shouldn't be retaining. Sometimes, we carry all kinds of trivia in our minds that sometimes I'm sure we wish we could just flush it all out of our system. But what we really need to feed our hearts and train our minds is God's word. In the midst of all the swirling information coming at us daily in the world, what we really need is the Word of God. Get into the habit of memorizing the Word of God so you can build up a rich reservoir.

Not only do you need to memorize God's Word, you also need to create a deep storehouse of memories so that you can remember what God has done for you in the past. God blesses us so many times and we thank God for the blessing and then move right on with our daily living forgetting all about the fact that God has blessed us. In those silent times in the middle of the storm, what you need is the ability to look back and relive where God has brought you.

Something written down that says "here is what God has done for me." We don't always need a fresh revelation but we need to remember how God has already brought you out. That time when the bill was due and you didn't know how you were going to work it out but you called up Customer Service and the rep said, "we'll just give you a grace period to give you a little more time to pay your bill." That time, when you had an urgent interview and you were running late and God made all the lights green! That time, when your body told you that something was wrong but after you came out of the MRI machine and the report was read, you learned that you didn't have any sickness.

That time, when your car broke down and you thought you were going to have to walk but God opened up a cheap rent-a-wreck and you were able to keep on rolling. Your faith was tested there because you had to consider whether you were going to ride the hoopty and worry about what other folks were going to say or were you going to get in that jalopy and ride it until it dies?

The first car that I ever bought was a Mercury Lynx. I purchased it in New Jersey before moving to Michigan and then on to Indiana. I truly believe that that car was given to me to test my faith because I always seemed to be in a storm with it. That Lynx just would not work consistently for me and so when I got to Indiana, the head gasket blew. This was a critical component of the car having something to do with the radiator. The cost of the repairs was going to be $2500. Funds I didn't have on hand at the time, so that car sat in the repair shop's parking lot for a long time.

One of my co-workers at Electronic Data Systems offered me a 1970s Catalina that he was selling for $100. You might not remember what a 1970s Catalina looked like but it was about 4 city blocks long or at least it appeared to be. One long bucket seat in the front and another in the back.

It was a HUGE vehicle and my coworker offered it to me for $100. Where are you going to buy a car and receive the title for $100? The other thing I was told was that the brakes were not totally up to snuff and that I needed to get them serviced as soon as possible. The car didn't look like much, but I drove it regardless of what other folks may have thought.

The brakes were so bad that when I saw a traffic light at an intersection half a mile away, I had to start stopping a quarter of a mile away way in advance of the color of the light at the intersection. If I even thought that the light was going to turn red I had to start preparing to brake because the brakes were so bad on the car. But you know what? It got me to work and it kept the paycheck coming so I could provide for my family and it got me where I needed to be.

When the going gets tough with my current vehicle I think back to how God took care of me many years ago with the Catalina and I just have to say, "Thank you Lord. I might not have looked good but you got me where I needed to go. Lord I might have had some problems before but when I was down, you had a way of lifting me up. When I didn't think I was going to be able to make it, you came right on through."

When it appears that God is silent, you better have a reserve. You better have a reserve of God's Word so you can say, "God is my refuge and strength. A very present help in the time of trouble" (Psalms 46:1). Even when you have to walk through the valley of the shadow of death, we need to remember that God is there with us. You have to have a reserve of God's Word coupled with a good memory so you can say "Lord, thank you for days gone by. When I didn't think I was going to make it but you brought me on through." The Psalms are a big diary of God's faithfulness on David's behalf through all of the storms in his life.

Recall in the Old Testament how the children of Israel had been defeated because of their disobedience and the temple was destroyed. In 2 Kings 22:8, the workers who were repairing the temple at King Josiah's command had this report, "I have found the Book of the Law in the temple of the Lord." The King and the people read through the scrolls and were reminded what God had done for their ancestors in days gone by. They recounted how God had brought them out Egypt; how God had parted the Red Sea; and how God had given them a standard for living lives that would be pleasing before Him.

Likewise, you need a written record of what God has done in your life so that you too can remember what God has done for you. Maybe you have never taken the time to write in a journal. Now would be a good time to start especially when God answers your prayers. You, like King Josiah, need to be able to look back on the great things

God has done for you in days gone by. You need that testimony when Heaven appears to be silent or the answers are slow in coming. The other benefit of keeping a journal is that you also are creating a legacy of God's faithfulness that you can pass along to future generations in your family. A journal becomes our memory and a testimony in the time of a storm.

When God is silent is there anything from which you can draw to encourage yourself or will you be running on an empty tank? Silence tests our memory.

Silence Challenges Our Status

Storms also have the ability of calling into question who you are or to whom do you belong. When storms come your way, the devil has a way of dropping propaganda in your ear to cause doubt to arise. Rev 12:10 says that the devil is ". . . The accuser of our brothers and sisters, who accuses them before our God day and night, . . ."

When the storms are coming and it seems like you aren't hearing anything from heaven, the devil will replace that silence with accusing words in your ear, "See, you call yourself a Christian and look, you're in this storm all by yourself. See how that God you say you serve has left you to fend for yourself."

Or other times, he will hit us through a girlfriend or a boyfriend, "Gurl!!! If I were you . . ." Isn't interesting when folks say that, "If I were you . . ." because if they were in that situation, they would never do what they are telling you to do. The "they" are quick to tell you what to do, but when they get into a situation of their own, they don't want to hear anything you have to say especially if they are not a believer. Some of them come along in YOUR storm and say, "If I were you, I would forget that church stuff. I know you go up there for prayer meeting and all that stuff but what is it doing for you now?"

If you are a believer who is following Jesus Christ, you have made sure that you are following Jesus and that He is on board your vessel (yes, even if He is asleep), just remember who you are. You are a child of the King. Remember the assurance that Jesus gave to us, "I give them eternal life and they shall never perish. No one can snatch them out of my hand."

Do you know who's hand you are in? You may remember the slogan of one insurance company, "You're in good hands." But as a child of God you don't want to be in the good hands of an earthly insurance company that could be here one day and gone the next. You should want to be safe in the arms of Jesus. You want Him to rock you in the cradle of His arms. Say to yourself that "I am a child of God." 1 John says that "everyone who believes that Jesus is the Christ is born of God" (1 John 5:1). Paul got excited in the later part of Romans 8 when he asked, "Who shall separate us from the love of Christ? Shall trouble or hardship or persecution or famine or nakedness or danger or sword?" (Romans 8:35) NO!!! None of those things can separate us from a loving God because we are more than conquerors through Him who loves us (Romans 8:37).

In the middle of a challenging situation, you need to recognize who you are. You need to remember your status. When we are going through something and it appears that God is silent, you have to trust Him. Even when you can't see your way, trust that God knows what God is doing. When friends fall by the wayside and the boat is taking on more water, trust him. When you have to lay your head on the pillow sometimes and cry yourself to sleep, trust Him. When it seems like the storm is getting more intense, trust

Him more and more. When friends laugh at you, trust Him. When close relatives get up next to you and give you the same advice Job's wife gave to him, "You need to just curse God and die," trust Him. Even when you are confused, trust Him.

Why? The hymn writer put it this way, "We are tossed and driven on the restless sea of time; somber skies and howling tempests oft succeed a bright sunshine; in that land of perfect day, (storms aren't going to last always; a time is coming when the storm will pass away) when the mists are rolled away, we will understand it better by and by.

I might be going through some things right now but I'm holding on. I'm trusting Him. In the middle of the storm is not the right time to jump out of the boat. When your boat is rocking back and forth that is not the time to get into the water. You and I have to trust him because you and I will understand it better by and by.

Job didn't understand why he went through the crisis that he did at the time but God is a great and wonderful God. When you look at Job at the end of the story, Job had twice as much at the end than he had when the story started.

We are often destitute of the things that life demands, want of food and want of shelter, thirsty hills and barren lands we are trusting in the Lord, and according to God's word, we will understand it better by and by. And don't miss the chorus: By and by, when the morning comes, when the saints of God are gathered home, we'll tell the story how we've overcome, for we'll understand it better by and by.

We need to trust God because God has brought you and I

a mighty long way. So, when you think about the goodness of Jesus, you have to admit that God has done some things for you. He's taught us how to trust Him; taught us how to slow down and remember all that He has done for us. God might be quiet for the moment, but I know that I'm still His child. I know that anything that comes to me has to go by Him before it gets to me. God is only going to allow so much to come my way.

So trust Him and recognize who you are. Storms are destined to come into our lives. It's not a matter of IF but WHEN. Sometimes, those storms put us in a silent period with God as we see in the text that Jesus was sleeping.

Jesus went through a period of silence even in his own life. Recall how Jesus wrestled in prayer in the Garden of Gethsemane struggling for the way by which salvation was to come into the world.

Remember, when Jesus was at Calvary on the cross dying for the sins of the world and how he cries out towards Heaven, "My God, my God, why have you forsaken me?" He was looking to Heaven and it was quiet, but Jesus never forgot who He was. Even though he felt forsaken, when Jesus took his last breath look at how he trusted in His Heavenly Father when he said, "Father, into your hands I commend my spirit."

Even when it seems like you are alone, you need to say, "Lord I'm in your hands." No matter what may come your way, you need to learn how to lean and depend on God. Because Jesus placed all of his trust and faith in His Father, the record shows that Jesus got up on Resurrection morning because even when Jesus was in a moment of silence, God was still with Him. God kept Him and God will keep you as well through the storm.

Jesus went through the silent treatment at Calvary, so that when you and I encounter the storms of life, we would have a Savior who not only is with us in the storm, but we have a savior who can bring us through the storm. Jesus has been through some storms of His own.

When we talk about the good old days, most of us had to go through some things in the "good old days." When we were going through the "good old days" they were not always so good. It was only after God brought us through winds and the rains that we could look back and say that they were "good old days."

There will be times when God is silent in your storm. Silence will test you; challenge your memory as well as your status but know that if you stay in the boat and remember the Jesus is on board, you WILL come forth as pure gold.

Prayer

Dear Lord we praise you this day for who you are. You are the God who created the heavens and the earth and so the storms that we encounter must be obedient to your will. While we do not always understand your ways and how you choose to operate in our lives, help us to hold up to those times when you delay in answering our prayers. When our faith is put to the test may we be found to be faithful disciples. It is our desire to pass the test the first time the storm comes our way. Give us a discerning spirit so that we might weather the storm. Give us the patience to understand that while we don't always understand everything here and now, we will understand things better bye and bye. Please touch our memories and prompt us to write down your good deeds and blessings that come to us on a daily basis so that we might have a rich testimony to review in those silent moments of our journey. Thank you

Lord for our status as your children before you. Though Satan loves to whisper accusation against us, may your Holy Spirit be a constant reminder and comforter in our lives so that we can walk in the assurance of who we are. We thank you today for the answers to prayer that are yet on the way. For it is in Jesus name that we lift these praises and petitions to you, Amen.

Reflection Questions

1. Have you experienced the silent treatment in your life from someone before? How did you deal with it?

2. Has there been a time in your life when it took God a long time to answer a prayer request? How did you resist the urge to take matters into your own hands to "help" God out? How did you respond when God declined your request rather than answering your prayer in the way you expected?

3. Do you have a treasure trove of scripture memorized for the Holy Spirit to draw upon in your life? What has been your biggest challenge in memorizing scripture? Is there a passage you lean on the most in your life?

4. Have you ever had doubts about your status before God? Why is it hard sometimes to carry the title "child of God"?

3 DEALING WITH FEAR

Word of the Lord found in Matthew 8:23-27,

> Matthew 8:23–27, 23 Then he got into the boat
> and his disciples followed him. 24Without
> warning, a furious storm came up on the lake, so
> that the waves swept over the boat. But Jesus was
> sleeping. 25 The disciples went and woke him,
> saying, "Lord, save us! We're going to drown!" 26
> He replied, "You of little faith, why are you so
> afraid?" Then he got up and rebuked the winds
> and the waves, and it was completely calm. 27 The
> men were amazed and asked, "What kind of man
> is this? Even the winds and the waves obey him!"

In this chapter our focus will be on verse 25, "The
disciples went and woke him, saying, 'Lord save us! We're
going to drown!'" Our emphasis will be on a subject area

that we all have to address at one point of our lives or another: "Dealing With Fear". As we have done in the previous chapters, our journey begins with prayer:

> "Gracious Lord we thank you now for your word. Your word is truth. Your word is a lamp unto our feet and a light unto our pathway. Heavenly Father I pray that in these next few moments that you would please move self out of the way and that your Holy Spirit would use this passage to strengthen the reader so that you might be glorified. There are times in our lives, dear Lord, when we are prone to exercise fear rather than faith. Teach us through Your Word to lean and depend on you rather than to focus on our circumstances. Increase our faith to trust you despite what our five senses might be informing us given the storm we might be in at the moment. Thank you Heavenly Father for what you are going to do in these next few moments we pray in Jesus name, Amen."

Have you ever been in a situation in your life where you were terrified? I'm not talking about a little shutter but a place where you were in the grip of fear and you didn't quite know what the end was going to be? I never will forget the time when I was living in the Detroit Metro area of Michigan. I had gone back to New Jersey for some occasion and was flying back to Detroit during the cold winter months and there was snow on the ground. Although I had flown many times to many destinations, on this occasion, it was the first time I was flying in a plane that required a landing when there was snow on the ground. Any other time when I had flown the weather had been nice, the plane landed and I had no thought about the process of landing the plane. But for some reason I could not quite get my mind wrapped around how this piece of metal that was flying at hundreds of miles of hour was going to land and stop on a snow covered runway.

Just as an aside, here in Florida where I currently reside the idea of ice and snow is a foreign idea or concept but if you have ever had to drive on top of ice (like many in the north eastern part of the United States), it is a horrible thing to step on the brakes of your car expecting the car to slow down or stop only to have the car keep on going.

On this particular winter evening, this plane was landing on a snowy runway and in the back of my mind I am wondering (almost praying), "How in the world, Lord Jesus, are You going to land this plane? There's snow and ice on the ground? I do not quite understand how you're going to do it." During the entire descent, I had taken up residence in a place called fear. I was praying really hard. I pray when I fly anyway but this particular time I was praying, "Lord, I don't know how you're going to stop this plane but it needs to stop without crashing." I was in the grip of fear.

Maybe as you are reading this you cannot relate to the ice and snow but if you've ever rode a rollercoaster ride you might understand what fear is about from a different perspective. Years ago when my two oldest children (daughter and son) were tweens (no longer kiddies but not yet teenagers), we attended an outing with my company to Hershey Park in Pennsylvania. For some reason (it must have been temporary insanity), I thought I wanted to get on a rollercoaster (which I normally don't ride). The coaster entitled The Great Bear was one of those rides where your feet dangle from the seat.

I studied the rollercoaster and watched it go through a couple of cycles from different points along the coasters path and I thought to myself, "That looks like it might be fun." I got in line and when my turn arrived, I sat down in the seat with my legs dangling. With those types of rides they don't put a seat belt on you but they drop what amounts to a full body harness that locks you into you seat so you cannot move. When the bracket dropped and I was locked into my seat, my heart started racing. And then the ride launched quickly and started climbing seemingly into the sky. Of course the law of nature is: whatever goes up has to come down.

And did it come down! The Great Bear not only came down it had loops that flipped you upside down. I would share more with you about this experience but I am unable to because as soon as they locked me into my seat, I closed my eyes and I knew nothing until I felt the ride stop!

There are moments in our lives when we do things that put us in places of fear and verse 25 of Matthew 8 shows the reaction of the disciples being in such a place. Jesus and the disciples were in the process of crossing over the sea of Galilee when a strong storm rose up on the water. It was fierce because the Bible says that water was coming into the boat. When you are traveling in a boat, it is critical that the water stay on the outside of the boat but in this case the water was coming over and in to the boat.

This had to be an unusual storm because we are not talking about just some casual boat cruisers here. We are talking about fishermen in the boat. Men who were used to being on the water. They had probably been through a storm or two before but here they were on the water and in fear of their lives. They were afraid of losing life itself.

Drowning is not a pleasant way to die. If I had my choice of death, drowning would be the last option I would select simply because you tend to be conscious of what is happening to you all the way until the end.

In the movie Pearl Harbor released in 2001, there is an event in that movie that occurs when the Japanese attack the USS Arizona and Oklahoma. The explosions cause each of those boats to flip over with the hull facing upwards and the upper decks under the water. There are scenes in the film where they show some of the men, still alive, underneath in the bottom hull of the ship. It shows how the water was rising and the men had no where to go and no way to escape. As the water arose, all they could do is anticipate their watery demise. Drowning is not a pleasant way to die and yet the disciples are in the middle of this storm and they are thinking that their boat is about to capsize.

What do you do when life's storms sweep into your life and they put you in a perilous situation? How do you deal with the fear that arises when it seems like the storm has the upper hand? Let's dig a little deeper to see how fear operates and what counter moves we can make to overcome its impact on our lives.

Fear Loves Ignorance

The main thing that fuels our fears is a lack of knowledge about a situation. If you stop and really think about the times when you have really been afraid in your life, what made you afraid was the fact that you did not know what was coming next. When you have knowledge, there tends to be less fear.

When the doctor tells us that we have cancer, we do not know what the treatment is going to be like. Sure folks who have been down that path might come alongside you and try to convey to you what is going on but until you actually go through it, you are not sure what the treatment is going to be like and you have no idea what the end is going to be.

When the car breaks down and requires $1000 worth of repairs and your emergency fund is depleted and you do not how you are going to get where you need to go, fear has a tendency to step right in with some negative answers. When you do not know how are you going to get to work come Monday, fear will stop along the way and pick up worry and make a visit to your residence. When that plane was landing on the ice and snow in Detroit, I didn't know how that plane was going to stop.

We are afraid when we are uneducated about a situation. To be truthful to the text, the disciples did not know Jesus that long. As we read this incident in the lives of the disciples, we know the end of the story already so we are aware of how Jesus operates. Put yourself in the disciple's shoes for a moment and then consider what this scene looks like from their perspective. Here you are in a boat in the middle of a tempest with someone you barely know who has gone to sleep in the middle of the storm.

Our story is in Matthew 8 and Jesus was just baptized in Matthew 3. He went through the temptations in Matthew 4 and then Matthew 5-7 is Jesus preaching His Sermon on the Mount. So we are not talking about a great deal of experience with Jesus at the time of our text. Fear has a way of creeping up on us when we don't know Jesus. When you don't know Jesus then you don't know how Jesus is going to operate in certain situations. You have to know Jesus in order to know how to operate when different storms arise in your life.

That's why combat soldiers go through drill after drill after drill for hours on end in peace time so that they get to know one another. Through those endless drills they get to know how they each operate, think and move. The last thing you want to do is to get on the battlefield and not know what your battle buddy is going to do. You don't want to be on the battlefield and turn to your field buddy for help and discover your help has run off somewhere because they are afraid.

When you don't know Jesus, you might be prone to take things into your own hands. And more times than not, our response is not going to be the same response as God. One of the ways we overcome our fears is to become knowledgeable about who Jesus is and how Jesus responds to different situations of life. That's what its important for the believer to be in Bible Study weekly and to be in Sunday School so you can get to know who Jesus is and how He moves; how He thinks; how He responds in various situations.

Look at the Sermon on the Mount in Matthew 5-7 to see all of the different ways Jesus tells us to respond to different situations. Jesus operates on the principle of loving your enemies. Hamas (the terrorist organization sworn to wipe out the nation of Israel) can you love Israel? Israel can you love Hamas? Republicans can you love Democrats. It's tough to love one's enemies and we do not always operate that way do we? But Jesus says, "The way I operate is to love one's enemies."

Jesus says in Matthew 5:37, "Let your yes but yes and your no be no." But we have people today who go to church who love to be in that grey area. They don't want to commit to Jesus all the way but want to keep one foot in the church and keep one foot in the world. Some folks are like the singer James Brown and are split all the way down to the floor trying to keep each foot in a different sphere. Jesus says let your yes be yes and your no be no.

When you are in a dispute, go and settle it before you get to the judge. In Matt 5:25-26 Jesus advises us to settle it before we go to court because when once the judge gets the case, a resolution will be out of your hands and the judge might give you a verdict that is less than satisfactory.

Learn how to operate like Jesus operates. He tells us in Matthew 6 to not do things to be seen and yet we live in a culture that loves to be seen. Everyone has a reality show on TV. Even you could end up in a reality show one day! With Periscope, one of the latest apps for your smartphone, anyone can broadcast their life experience across the internet for everyone to see. People loved to be seen. Everyone wants to have their 15 minutes of fame. But Jesus instructs us to do things such that the right hand does not know what the left hand is doing. And the beauty of Jesus wisdom is that even though we might not be seen, God will reward us openly.

If we are going to overcome fear we have to become knowledgeable about how God operates. We have to develop God mindset. When our young people go to school they need to get all the schooling that they can get and afford. They need to develop their brains to the maximum. Booker T Washington had no idea how he was going to get from West Virginia to Hampton, Virginia. But he knew one thing: "I've got to get an education. Don't know what it's going to take but if I have to walk the whole way I'm going to walk."

Booker T Washington got to Richmond and didn't have a place to stay so he slept underneath the raised wooden sidewalks. He went through all of that because he wanted to get an education. He understood the importance of developing his mind and his thinking. When we know something about Jesus and how He operates and we develop our minds as best we can, fear has a way of fading off to the side. We need to be students of God's Word because when His word gets on the inside, at some point it has to come out on the outside. As you live out your life in the Lord based upon what you have learned, your faith grows bigger and bigger.

If you are reading this and you've walked with the Lord for a while, do you run into anything now in your life that years ago would have wiped you out? But now you look at what used to be a challenge to you and you just laugh because it is so minuscule and trivial in the grand scheme of things. Your faith has grown to the point where you can say to the devil, "get out of my face". Fear loves for folks to be ignorant. He loves for us to be in the dark and when that happens, fear can flourish.

Fear Loves Isolation

Part of the problem with the disciples was not only did they not know Jesus that well, they were in the middle of a mess and they felt isolated. They were out in the middle of the Sea of Galilee and there was no quick stepping out of the boat and getting to dry land. They were cut off from the land by the expanse of the sea.

If you have ever been on a cruise before then you know what that feeling is like. When you go down to the cruise terminal in downtown Tampa and look at the Carnival or Royal Caribbean ocean liners, they look pretty big in port. But when you get out into the ocean, that ship that looked huge in port is merely a dot in the ocean. Even as big as they are, they are still subject to the winds when they start blowing. They too are liable to start swaying back and forth given a strong enough gale.

When you are dealing with a storm in your life, the devil loves to isolate believers on their own. Remember what Peter wrote in his epistle that the devil moves around like a roaring lion looking for someone to devour. I've watched enough Smithsonian and National Geographic TV programs to know that when lions go on a hunt they don't just jump out there and start running after any animal they see. They take their time and get down into a crouch. Sometimes they are in the high grass and you don't even see what they are doing. They don't go after the fastest animal in a herd or pack. I heard a comedian say that when you come upon a dangerous animal in the jungle, I don't have to worry about outrunning the animal, I just have to outrun you. Lions when they are hunting are looking to pounce on the young or the sick and feeble. In other words, she is looking for the weakest link to attack.

When you are in the midst of the storm, the worst thing you can do is to pull away from God or God's people. As a pastor, I have seen incidents where people encounter some gale force winds in their lives and they start to pull away from the church rather than drawing closer.

But if we expect believers to draw closer, our churches need to be safe and protective fellowships where we can be real and honest with one another. Sometimes the reason why people pull away is because when they try to be real in prayer chains and circles and open up about some of the deep things going on in their lives, rather than praying for one another, some individuals go around trash talking about others. We need to be the people of God where folks can be real with the hurts they are experiencing and have the expectation that someone is going help them with their heavy load. Galatians 6:1 admonishes us, ". . . if someone is caught in a sin, you who live by the Spirit should restore that person gently." Each person in the body of Christ has the obligation to look out for other believers in the fellowship.

On Sunday morning when we come into the house of God, people coming into the worship service hurting from the previous week's challenges and satanic attacks and traps. They haven't come to church to play or for foolishness but have come to be with God's people who can (or should) help when the going gets unbearable.

You and I need to be careful that when things are going bad, we too do not pull away. Recall that Elijah had a great victory on Mt Carmel against the prophets of Baal. God came down and swallowed up all the wet wood offering that was on the altar. In the end, Elijah set to flight all of those Baal prophets but the record also shows that just after that victory, Queen Jezebel got on Elijah's trail. She chased him so bad that Elijah fled to a cave existence. God gave Elijah a mighty victory on Mt Carmel but soon thereafter it was as if God went silent on Elijah and he had to hold up in a cave. In fact Elijah so despaired of life that he said, "Lord take me out of here."

David was on the run from King Saul and ran so far that David fled to the enemy of Israel—the Philistines—and determined that the best place for him to hide was among the enemies of God's people. Initially when Dave was on the run, he too was isolated and alone.

When we think about the Lord's table, we are reminded of Judas betrayal. After Judas had made the despicable bargain with the religious leaders to betray Jesus, Judas spiraled into a deeper mess because he refused to come back to Jesus and the disciples afterwards and confess his wrongdoing. Don't you think that Jesus would have forgiven him? Of course he would have (see Peter's reinstatement in John 21:15-21 following Peter's denial of

Christ). But Judas isolated himself and the devil began to pounce on his spirit convincing him that it was time to check out. The Bible record shows that Judas went out and hung himself.

Fear was able to take hold of the disciples as they traveled on the high Sea of Galilee because they were outnumbered by the swirling waters. Storms are easier to ride out if you have some other folks that can come along side you. That's why Hebrews 10:25 tells us not to give up meeting together as some are in the habit of doing. You may be reading this book right now and you know do not go to church on a regular basis. That pattern needs to change starting today! Even if you do not stand in need of something on a given Sunday, there is a high probability that someone in the fellowship needs to borrow some of your strength to make it through another week. The body of Christ gathers on the Lord's day in the Lord's house so that we can encourage one another and refocus our vision on the God who is able to do all things but fail.

Paul in 1 Corthinians 12 says that the body is a single unit even though it is made up of many parts. When you are not a part of the body on the Lord's day, there is a body part missing. Have you ever seen a handicapped person who was missing a body part? It looks out of place doesn't it. The handicap tends to make us feel uncomfortable.

Many of our armed service members from the middle eastern wars in Iraqi and Afghanistan suffered injuries that cost them arms and legs. When we see the veteran commercials on television the images can be disturbing because we expect the human body to be whole.

During one my mission trips to Malawi, the team once encountered an artist who did some beautiful paintings even though he had no hands. He has shortened arms that are just a bit below the elbow. As a youth he was caught stealing and the punishment for the crime was cutting off of his hands. He is missing body parts that left him physically incomplete.

When you are not regularly in church on the Lord's day, a body part is missing and to be missing a body part is not a good thing. Jesus tells us in John 15 that He is the vine and you and I are the branches. If we abide in Jesus and Jesus abides in us, much fruit will be produced because separated or apart from Christ, we can do nothing. Remember that fear loves to get us to a place where we are isolated and are cut off from all of our options.

Fear Has To Submit To Prayer

Fear will back up when confronted with prayer. Where do we see that in this story of the disciples on the storm seas? All you need to do is to look at what the disciples did after the water started coming into the boat. Remember that Jesus is asleep. The first things the disciples did was go to Him! They sought Jesus out in the midst of the storm. They woke Him up and then talked with Him as though He could do something that only God could do. If that's not prayer, I don't know what else that could be. We used to sing, "Have a little talk with Jesus. Tell Him all about your troubles. He will hear your faintest cry and answer bye and bye. Hear a little prayer wheel turning. Know a little fire's burning. Just a little talk with Jesus makes it right."

Why does fear have to submit to prayer? Two things happen when we pray. First, when we pray we are acknowledging our own limitations. We are saying, "Lord, I can only do so much." Sometimes it's hard for us to get to that place, isn't it? In the United States, we are blessed with so many different options when it comes to solutions to problems that it is challenging for us to say that we are limited in any way. But there are some challenges we run into that we have to admit are just too big for us to handle. Prayer says that we know out limitations.

Second, we acknowledge in prayer our dependence upon Almighty God. With God, all things are possible. When you go on your knees do you believe that? Or are you just throwing up some words towards heaven and hoping that something sticks? Prayer has a way of sustaining us through the storms of life. Have you been through some storms?

Jacob was going through a storm. He thought his brother Esau was coming to wipe him out. But prior to meeting Esau, Jacob wrestled with the Lord. He didn't know what was going to happen to him tomorrow but he found himself wrestling with God and was determined that he wouldn't let God go until God blessed him.

Sampson found himself blind and without the strength that made him famous and feared among the Philistines. From a position of being chained, he cried out to God and had an honest talk with God. "Lord, I know I messed up, but Heavenly Father if you just give me one more chance, allow your Holy Spirit to fill me one last time and I will take out these Philistines and be obedient to you all the way till the end."

Jonah found himself in the belly of the large fish. He had been in a storm of his own that resulted in him being thrown overboard and swallowed by a large fish. In the belly of any animal is not a place any of us would like to be and if we were there, we too would definitely be praying! For three days and three nights Jonah took up residence in that fish's belly. After a three day prayer meeting, the fish spit Jonah out onto dry ground.

We know what prayer can do when we look at the life of Daniel who found himself in the den of lions. He was in a tempest. In fact prayer is what got him in the storm in the first place. Prayer not only put Daniel in the lion's den but it kept him when he got there. Prayer even converted the king. The king that put Daniel in the den came the next morning and asked, "Daniel has the God that you serve been able to keep you? Has He made a way for you?" Don't you just hear Daniel saying, "Yes king, I had a good night's rest last night. I know you didn't sleep well last night but I slept comfortably on the lion's mane." Prayer has a way of moving situations.

One of my favorite choirs of all time is the Brooklyn Tabernacle Choir and they sing a song, "All the way from Calvary He prayed for me, He prayed for me, He prayed for me. All the way from Calvary He prayed for me. He died to set me free." When you look at the path that Jesus took heading to the cross you see prayer being exercised throughout the journey. In the garden of Gethsemane Jesus went through an agonizing prayer session with the Father. He wrestled with what was going to take place at Calvary. "Lord, if it be your will, . . ." was Jesus exclamation. He prayed so hard that the water in his sweat was replaced with blood. "Lord, if it be your will let this cup pass from me yet not as I will but as you will."

Prayer has a way of displacing fear. Even when the Romans were attaching Jesus to the cross at Calvary, what were Jesus words? "Father, forgive them." That's a prayer. Jesus prayed for them because they didn't even know what it was they were doing. Even when Jesus time on the cross had come to a close, look at what Jesus did, "Father, into your hands I commend my spirit". You cannot be in better hands than God's hands no matter the situation may be.

Look at what God did for His son. Jesus went to the grave after Calvary on Friday but on Resurrection Sunday morning, Jesus got up with some power. Jesus didn't display a whole lot of power on Friday but when He arose on Sunday, the Bible says that he got up with All power over death, hell and the grave.

I do not know what calamity you might be in at the moment but when fear raises up, I'm going down. I'm going down on my knees in prayer. Fear might have me on shaky ground but prayer says in this will I be confident: "I will see the goodness of the Lord in the land of the living" (Psalms 27:13)

Fear might say that God is moving too slow and that I had better get up and handle the situation myself but prayer tells us to "Wait on the Lord and be of good courage and He will strengthen your heart." Fear will say that you had better stop being goody two shoes and get yours while you can get it. This turn the other cheek stuff is for the birds and you had better turn the enemy's cheek with your hand. But prayer says that we're going to be steadfast, unmovable, always abounding in the work of the Lord for we know that our labor is not going to be in vain (1 Corinthians 15:58).

Fear might ask the question: Who is this God that you worship? Can He really come through? Prayer responds, "Who is the King of Glory? The Lord strong and mighty. The Lord mighty in battle" (Psalms 24:8). Who is the King of Glory? Fear will say that Jesus is asleep, leave him alone. But prayer says, "My God never sleeps. He that keeps Israel neither slumbers nor sleeps" (Psalms 121:4). If God is going to be up all night, there is no need for both of us to be awake!

No matter what situation you are in, prayer will keep you. When your load gets heavy, prayer can lighten the load. When your friends turn their backs on you, prayer reminds you, "What a friend we have in Jesus, all of our sins and griefs to bear." When your heart is broken, prayer has a way of mending the broken and crushed heart. When you feel all alone, bear in mind that God is right there with us even though you may have to walk through the valley of the shadow of death. Know that God is right there with you. When you feel like you are over your head, prayer has a way of throwing us a life preserver such that you might be able to hold up.

When you feel like you're about to faint, prayer will prop you up. And not only will prayer prop you up but prayer can take you to higher heights. When your enemy thinks that you are done and defeated, David at the close of Psalms 23 says that God will "prepare a table before me in the presence of my enemies." Other folks might have thought you were wiped out and then they look around and see you sitting at the welcome table. God has made a way out of no way!

Please come to grasp the power of effective prayer. Don't just talk about prayer but make it a part of your everyday walk with the Lord. Make sure that you are in a prayer meeting each week in your local believer's fellowship. Make prayer a priority in your life. If we are going to make it through the storms of life; if you're going to deal with fear, prayer has got to be a part of who you are.

We have to go to Jesus because He's got the answer. Jesus is THE answer for any storm through which you might have to ride. Does he have the answer for you? Jesus is not only the answer but Jesus also has the answer for your situation, time and place. Jesus is able to do something.

When we come to God in prayer, you have to come believing and trusting that when you pray, God is going to be able to do something with those prayers.

Fear is real. All of us have to deal with fear at some point in our lives. Some people when they get into a fearful situation choose to pitch their tent and remain in that region. They take up residence in the camp of fear. Only when we understand who Jesus is can we be set free from that camp.

Do you understand that you are God's child? When you are God's child, folks have to be careful what they do to you. It's a fearful thing to put your hands on one of God's children. What is your reaction when someone does something to one of your children? Do you just play it off and think nothing about it? I don't think so! Most times we get up into someone's face about the situation. Is God going to do anything less? When one of God's children are touched, God is not going to do any less. The devil has to be careful when he stretches out his hand onto God's child.

When fear comes our way, we have to get knowledgeable. We have to know God's word. Jesus said that we should know the truth and the truth will make you free (John 8:35). Too many are in bondage today because we don't know God's word. But when the knowledge of God's Word takes root in your life, a whole different perspective on life will open up to you.

Fear wants you to be alone and isolated. The devil can beat you up no matter how strong you think you are when you are all alone. Your strength in comparison to the strength of the devil cannot hold up so the devil loves to get you by yourself. But you need to stay in the fellowship of the saints. No matter what you are going through, you need to be determined to be in someone's house of worship on the Lord's Day. We've got to be around God's people. God designed things that way for no matter where we go regardless of what state or what city we might visit, there you will find some of God's people.

You can find some of God's people everywhere even if they don't look like you. Even if they don't talk like you the Spirit of God can rest between two or three folks that have gathered together in God's name. And if God is in the midst of God's people then that is a place where you can draw some strength.

Fear loves to keep us isolated but you just stay on your knees because trouble has to back up when prayers start going up. Maybe you don't understand the storm that you are going through but you just say, "Lord, you are my refuge and my strength. A very present (that means right now) help in the time of trouble." We need to learn how to lean on the Lord when the storms of life start raging. Prayer unlocks the door that keeps us in constant communication with Almighty God.

The devil loves to trick us. He has us fearful of stuff in the world. Who we really need to be fearful of is God Almighty. If you want to have some fear, we should have fear about not doing what God has asked us to do. You may have grown up in a household where if mother asked you to do something, you didn't get a second chance to hear what it was that momma told you to do. You had a healthy fear because if momma or daddy told you to do, you just needed to get up and do it.

The devil has us fearful of a lot of stuff that is happening in the world and we should not give a second thought to the things that God said we should be afraid of. What we need to be mindful of is whether we have done what God has asked us to do. The Bible reminds us that we all have to appear one day before the judgement seat of Christ. And we'll have to give an account of the life that we have been living. It is appointed upon us once to die and after that the judgement. But if you have Jesus on the inside and He is your personal Lord and Savior then you'll not only do what you have been tasked to do but you'll also share in His glory in the world to come.

Reflection Questions

1.   Name an experience in your life when you were really, really afraid of something, someone or some situation.

2.   Fear can cause us to either fight or flight. Can you think of a time when fear caused you fight? How about a time when fear cause you to flight?

3.   What are some of the reasons why believers don't share their fears with other believers in the body of Christ? What are the barriers to sharing?

4.   In Joshua 1, the Hebrews were getting ready to cross over into new territory. Joshua is leading the people by himself without backup from Moses. What were some of the encouraging words that God gave to Joshua to help alleviate his fears?

5.   What are some of the passages or stories from God's word that give you strength and assurance when fear and anxiety choose to raise their heads? Why are these passages so dear and

important to you?

4 JESUS SAVES

The Word of the Lord found in Matthew 8:23-27,

> Matthew 8:23–27, 23 Then he got into the boat
> and his disciples followed him. 24 Suddenly a
> furious storm came up on the lake, so that the
> waves swept over the boat. But Jesus was sleeping.
> 25 The disciples went and woke him, saying,
> "Lord, save us! We're going to drown!" 26 He
> replied, "You of little faith, why are you so
> afraid?" Then he got up and rebuked the winds
> and the waves, and it was completely calm. 27 The
> men were amazed and asked, "What kind of man
> is this? Even the winds and the waves obey him!"

In this chapter our focus will be on v. 26, "'You of little faith, why are you so afraid?' Then he got up and rebuked the winds and the waves, and it was completely calm." We will be examining the topic, "Jesus Saves". Let us pray. "Gracious Lord, we thank You now for Your Word. Your word is truth. Gracious Lord I pray that Your Holy Spirit would empower these words that your reader is about to partake. Someone right now may be in the midst of the storm; someone might be looking at a storm that is coming over the horizon. We pray that You would minister to us even right now.

In August, 2014 something unusual happened out in the Pacific around the Hawaiian Islands. The Aloha state was bombarded with not just one hurricane but two. They came one right behind the other. These storms caused havoc disrupting people who were going to work and to students who were going to school. These hurricanes even effected those who had come as tourists to the Aloha State. When storms come into your life they have a way of messing up your normal routine. As we have explored in the previous chapters, there are times in our lives when storms of various degrees are going to blow. When these storms blow, they are going to try to bring as much havoc as possible.

Storms have a way of coming without warning. Have you ever gone into the grocery store with it being sunny outside, but then as you are coming out, the heavens have opened up and rain is falling like cats and dogs while you are stuck without an umbrella?

Storms don't always announce when they are coming. When they do come into our lives, we get on our knees and lift up our voices in prayer. Sometimes it seems as although God doesn't hear us. "Lord, I need an answer right now. Before I even get done with this prayer, it would be alright if you answered me." God doesn't always operate that way does God? If we focus our attention on the storm rather than on Jesus, fear has a way of setting in and begins to play with our emotions and even our faith. The thing we have to remember about a storm is that all storms have an expiration date. When you go to the store and you buy milk, do you not check the expiration date on the container? That date represents the last date that the grocer can sell the milk in the store. Once that date has been reached, the milk must be taken off of the shelf and is no longer able to be sold. Storms are the same way. They may come and have a lot of variety. Some may even stir up a whole lot of stuff, but I have never heard of a perpetual storm that never ends. A tempest is going to come, it is going to blow and then it is going to fade away. This storm in Matt 8 has just about reached its expiration point because Jesus is getting ready to respond to what has been happening up to this point in this journey. Let us see what we can learn when Jesus takes action.

Our Faith Is Supposed To Grow

God allows storms to come into your life many times to test us and to see just how strong we are. The winds are supposed to make us a little bit stronger. Jesus wakes up and gets on the disciple's case saying, "You of little faith." Just as a little child progresses through the growth stages at school, the believer is also supposed to grow and mature in their faith.

Paul in Colossians 1, "And we pray this in order that you might live a life worth of the Lord and may please him in every way bearing fruit in every good work. Growing in the knowledge of God." If you are reading this and have just come into the household of faith as a babe in Christ, you are going to be treated differently because you are a baby. Babies are not handled the same way as adults. Ultimately, you are expected to grow from being a babe into a fully grown adult believer.

Paul also says, "We ought to always thank God for you my brothers and rightly so because your faith is growing more and more and the love each one of you have for each other is increasing." Jesus chided the disciples not for having a lack of faith but for having "little" faith. He acknowledged that they had some faith but that it was little. They trusted too little.

A couple of times in the gospels, Jesus remarks about the disciple's little faith. In Matthew 14, we see Peter walking on the water toward Jesus but as soon as he took his eyes off of Jesus and focused on the turbulent waters below him, he began to sink. Jesus remarked, "Peter, why do you have such little faith" (v. 31).

Just prior to the above episode in Matthew 14, Jesus had been ministering to a large group of people and the crowds had tarried with Jesus all day. At the end of the teaching lesson, the master turned to the disciples and asked them to give the crowd numbering some five thousand people something to eat. The disciples got all frustrated and wondered, "How in the world are we going to feed all these folks? If we had a year's salary we couldn't take care of all these folks." Jesus again tells the disciples that they have "little" faith.

Jesus gets on their case for having "little" faith. More than likely if you are reading this book, you at least have saving faith (if you don't even have that, turn to the appendix and see how you can change that immediately). Saving faith is faith that is enough to trust Jesus for your salvation and to know that you have a reservation already secured for eternity.

Saving faith is not enough. God is looking for some disciples who are willing to grow their faith. Someone who is willing to go through some storms and then come out with a faith that is stronger than when entering the storm. You might be feeling the strong breezes of a storm right now as you are reading this book. If you come out of the storm the same way that you went in to the storm, then you will have missed an opportunity to grow and strengthen your faith.

Never waste a storm opportunity that comes your way. Lost your job? That's a storm opportunity. Relationship on the skids? That's an opportunity to get stronger. Saddled with a load of debt that you don't know how its going to be paid? At that moment class is in session. Right now is the time to grow and get stronger. Did you say some things that kicked up a storm of gossip? This is your chance right now to grow.

When your faith grows stronger and you've gone through some storms; when you've come through some storms, you can then embrace what James is talking about in James 1:2-4, "Consider it pure joy my brothers whenever you face trials (when we are going through a storm we hardly ever consider it a joyous time) because you know that the testing of your faith develops perseverance; perseverance must finish its work so that you may be mature and complete, not lacking anything."

Look at that progression: trials and testing brings about perseverance. When I was growing up sometimes the storms would come and mom would say, "turn off that light; turn off the television; get yourself a nice chair somewhere and sit down." The storm might be flashing and my brother and I would want to go out to play or move around, but we had better not even think about getting up and moving around. When the storms came it built up perseverance in us. Why? Because we had to sit down and wait for the storm to pass on over.

When perseverance comes, we grow a little bit and mature. When you are mature, then James tells us that we are complete. So, faith is supposed to grow but that doesn't happen on its own. When momma pushes you out of the womb and brings you into this world, the growth in us begins and is automatic. You don't have to think about growing. Growth just happens. In the Christian faith if we want to grow it is going to take some effort. Seniority in the church doesn't automatically mean you have growth. You've got to get into the word. You have to read your Bible. When you go to the Lord's house you need to come with your own Bible, a highlighter and a pen so you can jot down some thoughts from the Spirit in the margins or on your bulletin. You should be a growing believer by reading God's word regularly.

Then when trials come and you go through experiences in life you can embrace them as growth opportunities. So, Jesus would have us to know that our faith is supposed to grow.

Why Be Afraid?

Jesus then turns to the disciples and asks them, "Why be afraid?" Jesus calls them on the carpet for their lack of trust. We need to get in our spirit that if we are going to do the work God has called us to do in his Word (and we have been called to do something in his Word), we have to lift up the name of Jesus. Jesus said that if He was lifted up, He would draw all men unto himself.

When we do the work that God has called us to do, we can have assurances that displace fear. Fear loves ignorance but when you have some knowledge and you've gone through some storms, you can have some assurances that when you are doing God's will. The forces of the enemy raise up to attack you, you can stand strong and say like the Apostle Paul, "If God be for us, who can be against us?" You can tell the devil to take his best shot but no matter what comes my way, I'm going to stay on the path that God chosen for me.

Jesus gives us that assurance by not only saying "Go" but as you do go, "Surely I will be with you always even to the end of the very age." When you know that Jesus is walking with you and you are in the center of His will, you can stand strong despite the hurdles and the obstacles of the enemy because you have the confidence that God's Son is right by your side.

So, Jesus is asking you and I to move forward. Just like he impressed upon the disciples, He is imploring us to go to the other side and you might need to go when it doesn't appear that makes sense. When things don't make sense, that can induce fear. It might appear that there is more ministry in our churches sometimes than revenue coming in. It might mean that you have to minister to folks that don't look like you or don't talk like you. Sometimes the ministry methods by which ministry was in the past might have to change for a new generation of the lost. Sometimes it seems like the government is becoming more hostile to those of the household of faith but rest assure that if Jesus says, "We're going to the other side" then you're going to get to the other side. If Jesus says that we are going to such and such a place, that is exactly where you're going to end up.

The disciples forgot who was on board. They forgot that when Jesus is on board, the winds can only do so much blowing. When Jesus is on board, the waves are only going to come so far. When Jesus is on board, the sky is only going to get so dark. When Jesus is on board, the lightning can only do so much. When Jesus is on board, some might sow tares but those tares are only going to grow so much. When Jesus is on board, some people might throw some rocks and try to hide their hand but that rock is only going to go so far. When Jesus is on board, weeping can only last for the night. When Jesus is on board, the devil can only go so far.

We need to make sure that Jesus is on board. Because if Jesus is on board . . .

Jesus Can Handle The Storm

As children of God, we don't have to be afraid and go to pieces. The disciples had little faith. Mustard seed faith. Thankfully for them and for us, it doesn't take a whole lot of faith. Mustard seeds are smaller than the sesame seeds we find on our favorite fast food sandwich. Just a little bit of faith can launch Jesus into action.

When the storm is at its fiercest, Jesus wants us to trust him. Don't you just hear Jesus saying, "I got this!" v. 6 records that, "He got up and rebuked the winds and the waves" and look what happened: it became completely calm. That original language translation of "got up" meant that Jesus "raised up". He was stirred up. Have you ever been stirred up? Have you been in a situation where you were calm one moment but somebody pressed your button and you raised up? That is what happened with the Master. Jesus got up from His sleep; from His restful slumber, and He got with the intent on doing something. Sometimes we get up all big and bad but we really aren't planning on doing anything. Some people talk a good game but when it comes time for fight or flight, they are on the first plane to the farthest reaches of the plant.

When Jesus got up, Jesus was intent on taking care of this situation. Jesus was not going to make a suggestion to the wind. Jesus was not going to negotiate with the waves, He was going to get up and take care of the situation. When Jesus gets up, you had better look out.

The New Century Version of v. 6 says that Jesus "gave the command." Jesus could give the command because He made the winds and the waves. Do you not hear Jesus saying, "Waves you cannot do anything to me. If it wasn't for me you would not even be here." Jesus could tell the thunder to get somewhere and sit down because He made the thunder.

When the storms of life blow across the bow of your ship, Jesus has the authority over that situation. Genesis 1:1 says, "In the beginning, God created the heavens and the earth." That means anything that comes after the word "created" is under the control and authority of Almighty God. The psalmist put it another way when he said, "The earth is the Lord's and the fullness thereof" (Psalms 27:1). That includes the world and everyone and everything within it.

Jesus has authority over the aches and pains that touch your body every now and then. Jesus has authority to make your checkbook stretch when there's more month than money. Jesus has the authority over your boss on the job. If you have a boss that is hard on you, don't argue with them but take that boss to Jesus because Jesus has the authority. Jesus has the authority over the devil and the traps that the devil tries to set. He has the authority over that vehicle that the mechanics said should have been dead a long time ago. You may be driving a vehicle that the mechanic said should have been put out to pasture a long time ago but you are still riding in style because Jesus has the authority. Jesus has authority over that wayward child that won't do right. Jesus even has authority over the White House, the black house and every other color house.

Jesus has authority over high blood pressure, low blood pressure and even no pressure at all. When He arose from the grave, He told His disciples in Matthew 28 that "All authority has been given unto me in heaven and in earth."

ALL authority means just that: ALL Authority. He has authority over the church house as well as that child that refuses to act right. He has authority over the cancer the doctor just told you about. There is no storm that can boldly stand up after Jesus speaks because Jesus has can handle any storm that may rise up in our lives.

He may not speak as quickly as we would like but that's where faith comes in. Paul in 2 Corinthians says that we "walk by faith and not by sight." This world is all wrapped up in what it can see. The world is concerned with the bling and stuff that sparkles. It is what we cannot see, many times, that has the greater value. And that's where our faith has to kick in.

So, when Jesus got up and exercised His authority over the winds and the waves, the text says that everything became completely calm. Not getting calm but that it was calm. When Jesus speaks things start to happen immediately. He doesn't say, "Peace get still" but "Peace, BE still." There is no storm that comes into our lives that is beyond God's ability to act. It may be beyond our ability to act. Might be beyond your opinionated friends who are always giving you unsolicited advice. Always remember, Jesus can save you in the midst of the storm.

Grow your faith my friend. Give Jesus something to work with when the going gets tough. Don't be the kind of Christian that shuns reading and studying God's word. Don't be the kind of believer that has no time for God when the sun is shining but when the dark clouds start to form in your life, you want God to bring ALL of God's resources to bear on your behalf. God has given us some tools through His Word. There are some storms we encounter where we already have all of the resources that we need to take care of the situation. There are some storms where the only thing we can do is to get on our knees and get before the Lord. There some storms where the Word and prayer don't carry us and we have to just say to the Lord, "I need you to please show up!" In those moments we can say like the psalmist, "God is my refuge and strength, a very present help in the time of trouble." Handling the storms of Life. Jesus has us covered. When He stands up, something is going to change. You might remember when you were going up that if you didn't do what momma and daddy told you to do, you can remember them saying, "You better pull it together." When my three oldest children were young and I they didn't do what I asked them to do over and over, I would stand up and because I stood up I was already moving. There was no negotiating at that point. Something was going to happen. When Jesus stands up, He's going to take care of the situation. He is going to deal with the storms.

You may be reading this and you have never thought about the fact that Jesus could help you with the storms you are going through in your life. You have been trying to get through them all by yourself and in your own strength. Jesus not only has authority over the tough, stormy situations in our lives but He also has authority over the sin debt you have accumulated. He has that authority because He gave His life on a rugged cross at Calvary. He stayed in the tomb after they took Him down from the cross and on the third day morning, Jesus arose from the tomb with authority over death, hell and the grave. If you've never given Jesus access to your life, now would be a good time to allow Him to come onto your boat and rescue you from THE storm that could claim your life for all eternity.

Reflection Questions

1. Reflect on how long you have been a believer.

What type of activities do you do on a regular basis to grow your faith?

2. What activities hinder your spiritual growth?

3. How have you used your stormy experiences to help others to grow?

4. What experience has happened in your life that taught you that Jesus can handle your storms?

5 LESSONS LEARNED

The Word of the Lord found in Matthew 8:23-27,
Matthew 8:23–27, 23 Then he got into the boat
and his disciples followed him. 24 Suddenly a
furious storm came up on the lake, so that the
waves swept over the boat. But Jesus was sleeping.
25 The disciples went and woke him, saying,
"Lord, save us! We're going to drown!" 26 He
replied, "You of little faith, why are you so
afraid?" Then he got up and rebuked the winds
and the waves, and it was completely calm. 27 The
men were amazed and asked, "What kind of man
is this? Even the winds and the waves obey him!"

Let us pray
"Gracious Lord we thank you now for your word.
Your word is jammed packed full of truth. Every
time we open it we learn something new about
who you are or what you desire of us. May your

> Holy Spirit use this book today to be a blessing to
> the reader. He/she may be going through
> something in their lives that only your word can
> address. I pray that you would touch right now in
> the precious name of Jesus, amen.

One of the things that I learned when I first started going
to seminary is that you and I are theologians. Even if you
have never gone to seminary and do not even have a
degree, you are a theologian. A theologian is someone
who talks about God. This definition of a theologian
came from my professor Dr Kortright Davis who defined
theology as follows, "A critical reflection of life in the light
of faith." It's nothing more than us thinking or reflection
upon our life in the light of the faith that we profess in the
Lord Jesus Christ.

As has been stated through this book, all of us have to go
through some storms at some point in our lives. After the
storm has past, sometimes we need to stop and just reflect
upon what just happened in the storm and is there
something that I can learn about who God is based on the
storm from which I have just emerged?

Many times we are just thankful to just get through the
storm. When the storm is raging, the boat is rocking back
and forth then Jesus calms the storm and we are on the
other side, sometimes we just want to say "thank you,
Jesus" and breathe a sigh of relief. But we need to stop
and reflect upon how God moved in the midst of the
storm. If we don't stop and reflect upon the test from
which we just emerged, we will miss the purpose and
lessons of the storm. As believers who are walking with
the Master, there are going to be those moments when we
are going to be tested.

Do you remember those occurrences when you were in

REV DARRYL M MATTHEWS

school and had to take a test and the results were less than spectacular (way less)? In some classes if I didn't do well, I would get a second chance to take the test so that I could do better the second time around. Taking a test a second time is alright in school but when it comes to our lives, it is better to learn something going through the storm the first time than to have to go through it a second time to grasp the lesson should have been learned the first time. I don't want God to have to retest me again with another storm.

As this book comes to a conclusion, let me encourage you to take some time to think about the storms you have been through and what lesson or lessons you should have learned from them. We'll do that in this chapter by examining the disciple's reaction to what just took place in the boat with Jesus. As we look at the disciples reaction to Jesus' calming of the storm, let's see if there is something they learned that would be useful to us in our walk (or ride) with the Lord.

Just to recap the story: the disciples were in the boat with Jesus. They are out on the water when the storm raised its ugly head. They experienced water pouring into the board over the sides while Jesus lay asleep through it all. They woke Jesus up and implored him to do something to keep them all from perishing. Jesus got and rebuked the disciples and asked them why they were all upset when He was on board. He told those waves, "Peace be still." The Word says that everything became completely calm. In this chapter's text, we see that after all had taken place, the disciples responded, "Wow, what manner of man is this?" In this chapter, we want to unpack the conversation the disciples had after Jesus arose from his slumber and dealt with the storm. What lessons can be learned and applied to our daily Christian living?

We Need To Appreciate What God Has Done

As children of a loving, great and generous God, we need to learn to appreciate more often what God has done and is doing in our lives. Notice the disciple's reaction to what Jesus had just done, "the men were amazed." Jesus had just demonstrated authority over nature by telling the storm to be still. If you don't think this was an amazing task, I would challenge you, during the next thunderstorm, to go outside and speak to the storm and drop me an email (stormyweather@vitallivingmedia.com) and let me know how that worked out for you (just be careful as you do it as I assume no responsibility for this experiment).

Jesus had just done something that was truly amazing and out of the ordinary. Imagine going out to the Howard-Franklin Bridge that spans between Tampa Bay and St Petersburg in Florida and standing in the middle of the bridge during a storm and telling the bay to be still and it actually became still! That's not something that you see every day. When you've gone through the storms of life and God has brought you out, do you ever come out with a sense of amazement and wonder about the God that we serve?

With television and the movies coming out of Hollywood, the visual effects are so realistic that it's hard for us to be amazed at things today. We are accustomed to seeing the spectacular on the big and small screens that we have become desensitized when we actually see something spectacular with our own eyes.

In the 1950s and 60s when Superman came on television, you could tell that the actor was not really flying and that it was fake. But to look at Superman in the movies today, you might just believe that a man could actually take off and fly. When you look at the movies coming out of Hollywood today, you might actually believe that dinosaurs are walking around on an island somewhere in South America. With the exception quality of the visual effects departments, you just might think there actually is a space ship somewhere that you could board and fly from one end of the galaxy to the other.

We have become so accustomed to all of the special effects in the media that we've gotten desensitized to the point where it takes more and more for us to be amazed. That desentization might blind us to the truly amazing things God has done or is doing in our lives.

If we are not careful as believers, we might get so accustomed to the blessings God sends our way on a regular basis that it can become hard for us to marvel at anything until a severe storm hits us.

Such is the case with many a believer in the United States and western civilization. We have been blessed with so much that we take things for granted. When I travel to Africa and I interact with brothers and sisters in Malawi, I am reminded how much we take things for granted. We take televisions, movies and other media for granted. One year during a mission trip to Malawi, we showed the Jesus film using a little video projector, a battery powered speaker and a movie screen made out of a white sheet secured to PVC piping. By our iPad/Phone and flat screen sensibilities, a rather primitive set up but you would have thought that Jesus had just walked into the village the way Africans responded to our little portable theater. They were amazed because it was something that they had never seen before.

Just like that example, the disciples were awe struck by what Jesus had just done. The Greek wording here says that they were "surprised." They were astonished and filled with wonderment. They came away with a sense of admiration for what Jesus had just accomplished. When was the last time God did something in your life and all you could say was "Oh my?" When was the last time God did something so stunning that all you could do is shake your head and say, "Go on Lord, you're just something else?" When was the last time you had some amazement over what God had done for you?

When God has moved in the midst of your storm, there ought to be some amazement that exclaims, "there is no God like my God." You need to stop and tell God, "I don't know what I would have done if you hadn't come through." It's the height of arrogance on our part for God to move on our behalf and then we just go on as if it was business as usual.

When God does something for you, don't be like the other nine lepers (Luke 17:17) whom Jesus healed who didn't stop to say "thanks." Jesus had sent them on their way and as they were going they discovered that their leprosy was gone! Only one turned back with a heart of gratitude to say "thank you." He acknowledged what God had done in his life.

These disciples were amazed at what had just taken place. When we go through brutal life weather, we need to learn how to appreciate God for all that God does. Do you realize that if God does nothing else for you that He's already done enough! The fact that God sent his only begotten son, Jesus, into the world to save you and that you have a ticket already booked for glory is a testimony to the fact that God has done enough for us already. Anything God has done for us beyond the salvation moment is bonus for us. We need to develop a spirit of appreciation. A spirit of amazement.

We Have To Ask The Right Questions

Questions have a way of getting us to think through some things. There are times when we do not like folks asking questions. We just want the answers or we just want someone to tell us what to do because we are intellectually lazy. Questions have a way of getting us to use that gray matter between our ears.

Keep in mind that we are in the early part of Jesus ministry and that the disciples are still getting to know Jesus. If you have grown up in the church with Sunday School stories about Jesus' miracles and God's Old Testament miracles, then you already know how God can work and has worked in the lives of God's people.

But this is all new to the disciples who are experiencing a miracle on this order for the first time. They ask a very appropriate question, "What kind of man is this?" He just calmed the storm. They wanted to know who in the world commands this kind of power? What country is he from? They knew that Jesus wasn't from around their vicinity with that kind of power. When someone calms the storms and the seas, that is power that we don't have. How many folks would love to have that kind of power? Would not it be nice when you were getting ready to go on vacation for you to be able to stay to a rising storm, "Give me two weeks before you blow?"

So, the disciples knew that the power that Jesus displayed was not power that came from the earthly realm. They were trying to figure out just who this person was that was in their midst. Even though Jesus had healed the sick previously in this chapter they had never seen anyone exercise control over nature. They were familiar with the Old Testament history where Moses and the children of

Israel got backed up against the Red Sea. They knew the story of how God blew open the Red Sea and the children of Israel were able to walk through on dry ground.

But it is one thing to hear a story about something amazing and something completely different when you experience it for yourself. They had heard stories of God's great power and how he rained down fire from heaven on Mt Carmel and swallowed up the wet and soggy sacrifice on the altar. They heard all about how Daniel was in the lion's den and God did another miracle in closing the lion's mouth but now they had seen a miracle for themselves. Answers are revealed to us many times through the storm. There are some things that we are not going to learn about God unless you go through the storm. You are not going to know how strong your faith is until you go through the storm. Some people would rather stay weak or small in their faith rather than grow stronger by going through a test.

So, the disciples ask the question, "What kind of man is this?" They recognized that the more you learn about who God is and the more you know about how God operates, the more you get to know God. When you get to know God, the closer you get in your relationship with him and that is always a good thing.

Can you say today that you have such a relationship with the Creator? Have you talked with the Father since church last Sunday? If you were in a marriage relationship and you only talked to your spouse on Sundays and did not converse during the week, what kind of relationship would that be?

If we are going to get the lessons learned from this storm event, you have to ask the right questions. Lord, what are you doing? What lessons are you trying to teach me? The

Psalmist says, "O Lord, our Lord, how excellent is your name in the all the earth". The more you know about who God is, the better off you will be in the long run. That's why the disciples were asking, "What kind of man is this?" They felt that they need to get to know this man because He has some power and a connection that they had not seen before.

Don't be the kind of believer who is content with wading in shallow water. When you get to know the great God that we serve, you learn there are some truly amazing things God wants to show you and share with you. But it only comes as you get to know God in the deep water that you learn certain God things. Going through the storm can bring about a closer walk with our God and that's a good thing even if the bad weather is not.

Experience Leads To Worship

Matthew, the writer of this gospel, is not trying to communicate in this text that Jesus will bring you out of the storm. That's not the central lesson of the text. Many times that is what people want to get out of this passage and apply to their lives but that is not the writer's aim. What Matthew is trying to get us to see is who Jesus IS. When we are more concerned about what God is doing for us, that is a focus on "US." But what we really need to understand when we are going through the storm is who God IS. A focus like the three Hebrew boys (Daniel ??) who realized that God might not rescue them but that God has the power to come to their rescue if God so chose.

Matthew is trying to get us to see just who Jesus is. He is Jesus, the Son of God. He may be, at the moment, wrapped in this human flesh with its limitations as demonstrated by the fact that Jesus was sound asleep, but

God does not need to sleep. The psalmist says, ". . . he who watches over Israel will neither slumber nor sleep" (Psalms 121:4). But Jesus was in this human flesh and he was in the hole of the ship sleeping because this physical body needs some rest when it gets weary. Even though Jesus was in the flesh, he was still all God and all man wrapped in the same package.

When you come through the storm and you see the hand of God move on your behalf because you are asking the right questions and pondering just who God is, you should come away with a Spirit of worship and praise for who God is and not just for what God has done for you.

Some folks can only praise God when God has done something for them or doing some miracle on their behalf. But if that is the extent of your worship—that you only worship God when He's done something for you—watch out. When you know who God is then your worship is going to be ongoing because God is the great I AM. He's always worthy of our praise. He's always worthy of us turning our face Heavenward and saying, "Holy, holy, holy is the Lord God Almighty."

In the Old Testament, folks were so in awe of who God is that they gave God some names. Maybe you can connect with one of those names. In the Old Testament they called him El Shaddai—Lord God Almighty. El elon— most high God. Adonai—Lord and Master. They called him Jehovah Shama—the Lord is there. They called him Jehovah Nissi—the Lord is my banner. Jehovah Rama— the Lord is my shepherd. Jehovah Rapha—the Lord is my healer (have you ever been healed?). Jehovah Jireh—the Lord will provide. Has he provided for you lately? Has God ever made a way out of no way?

He was called Jehovah Shalom—He is our peace. When

the storms of life are raging, I can lay my head on the pillow because Isaiah says that God will keep us in perfect peace when our minds are stayed on him (Isaiah 26:3). He's been called Jehovah Seraph—the Lord of hosts.

John in the New Testament didn't want to be outdone by his Old Testament writers so by the time he had finished penning his gospel and the epistles to the churches, he had a couple of names for the Lord as well. They called him King of Kings and Lord of Lords. They called him, Alpha and Omega, the beginning and the end. He was referred to as the first and the last. They called him the Lion of the tribe of Judah. He was called Immanuel—God is with us.

God will be with us when we call Him Light of the World. He said He was the way, the truth and the life. He is called the only begotten of the Father. They called him the Lamb of God. Jesus told Mary and Martha at the foot of Lazarus' tomb that they can call Him the resurrection and the life. Jesus knew that he was going to give him life on the cross at Calvary but He also knew that He was going to get up. Jesus wants us to worship Him because of who He is—He's got all power over death, hell and the grave.

When we get done praising Jesus on this side (we're just practicing right now); when we give up the walks of this life and we get into the presence of Almighty God, we'll be saying, "How did I get over?" Lord, you are worthy of all praise. The hymn writer put it this way, "All hail the power of Jesus name, let angels prostrate fall. Bring forth the royal diadem and crown Him Lord of all."

We're going to have to go through some storms in the earthly life. Are you going to get the lessons of the storm? Learn to appreciate God. For everything that God does on your behalf, you should learn how to say "thank you." Even down to the simplest things learn how to say "thank you." When you go to the store and the item that you want is on sale or it is buy one get one free, learn to just say thank you because isn't that how God works on behalf of God's children? He'll not only stretch your dollar to get one item but He'll throw in a second one for free.

When you're traveling over the highway and you're in a rush and the lights are all green along your path, say "thank you Lord". When God keeps you on the job that you have even in the midst of people getting laid off and caught up in reductions in force, learn how to say "thank you." You have less seniority than some folks who are getting pink slips and God continues to keep you, learn to say "thank you."

Learn to question. When you are going through the storm, just ask God, "What are you trying to teach me Lord?" or "Jesus, what are you trying to say to me?" Don't go through a storm in your life and miss the lesson that God is trying to teach you.

When you go through the storm and you come out on the other side, you should be a deeper worshiper of who God is. Don't worry about what God has done because God is always going to be active. Learn to worship God for who God is. Get in the habit of worshipping God for who God is. God said "I am that I AM". Not the "I Was" or "I Will Be" but he's the great "I AM" which means that God is right now! The Psalmist says that God is "a very present help in the time of trouble" (Psalms 46:1)

Never let a storm go to waste. Each one that comes our way has a purpose and in the end we should come out of the storm closer to the Lord. Maybe you are going through a hurricane right now and have no idea who God is or who God's son might be. This same Jesus that is in this stormy text you read earlier has taken some steps that you might know who He is. He died on the cross for your sins and all you have to do is say, "Jesus, I'm a sinner and I need you to come into my heart, clean me up, fix me up, fill me with your Holy Spirit." If you'll do that, He will come in and have fellowship with you and He will walk with you not just in the sunshine but also in the rain.

When Jesus is on the inside, the storms can rage; the devil can throw everything and the kitchen sink at you but Jesus will keep you. Even if Jesus doesn't calm the storm, He will keep you in the midst of the storm such that you come through alright.

Reflection Questions

1. If you were to look back over your life, what are the major milestones where you can see that God has moved in your life for which you are most grateful?

2. In the Old Testament, people would erect stones as a memorial to what God did at a certain place and time. What tools or process do you use to remember the major movements of God in your life (e.g., diary/journal, photos, etc)?

3. When was the last time you did a self-evaluation of where you are in the spiritual life? Are you cruising through life or stretching yourself so that you continue to grow?

4. Have any of the storms you've been through brought you closer to God? How is that closer relationships reflected in your daily walk and in your service to the Lord?

STORMY WEATHER

ABOUT THE AUTHOR

Rev Darryl M Matthews is an associate pastor at the First Baptist Church of College Hill in Tampa FL. He is a committed husband to Jowancia; a loving dad to Crystalyne, Jonathan, Christopher, Thomas and Luke; a doting granddad to seven children; a certified openwater SCUBA diver; professional photographer; and an award winning video producer & editor.

Since 2010, Rev Matthews has been a missionary to Malawi where he preaches the Good News and shares the gospel in villages throughout the warm heart of Africa. In 2015, he and Jowancia founded the 501(c)3 non-profit Africa Living (www.africavitalliving.org) to dig wells, provide school desks and distribute solar lights to students.

He is committed to building, motivating and communicating the Christian faith with and through the body of Christ and does this not only through his writing, teaching & preaching ministry but also through his daily online video broadcasts. His teaching ministry exists to encourage the body of Christ and equip believers to live out their faith everyday.

You can discover more information about Rev Darryl Matthews at www.pastordarryl.com.

REVIEW REQUEST

If you enjoyed this book and found it useful in the spiritual life, I would be very grateful if you'd post an honest review. Your support really does matter and it really does make a difference. I do read all the reviews so I can get your feedback and I look forward to making changes in future editions of this book as a result of that feedback.

If you'd like to leave a review then all you need to do is go the review section on the book's Amazon Page. You'll see a big button that says "Write a customer review"—click that and you're good to go!

Thanks again for your support

Yours in Christ

Rev Darryl
revmatthews@stormyweatherbook.com

Link to book's Amazon page: www.amzn.to/2qhEY2N

If you will write a positive review of my book on Amazon and email me a screen shot of your review, I will send you the first chapter of my next book (based on The Book Of Ruth) for FREE when it is available later this year.

www.ingramcontent.com/pod-product-compliance
Lightning Source LLC
Chambersburg PA
CBHW051044030426
42339CB00006B/191